NDIC PRESS
NATIONAL DEFENSE INTELLIGENCE COLLEGE

Finding Leaders

Preparing the Intelligence Community for Succession Management

Occasional Paper Number Seventeen

E. L. Hatfield
NDIC Research Fellow

NATIONAL DEFENSE INTELLIGENCE COLLEGE
WASHINGTON, DC

July 2008

The views expressed in this publication are those of the author and do not reflect the official policy or position of the Department of Defense or the U.S. Government.

NDIC PRESS

The National Defense Intelligence College supports and encourages research on intelligence issues that distills lessons and improves Intelligence Community capabilities for policy-level and operational consumers

Finding Leaders: Preparing the Intelligence Community for Succession Management, E.L. Hatfield.

Occasional Papers present the work of faculty, research fellows, students and others whose research on the intelligence enterprise is supported or otherwise encouraged by the National Defense Intelligence College. Occasional Papers are distributed to Department of Defense schools and to the Intelligence Community, and unclassified papers are available to the public through the College's web site at *http://www.ndic.edu.*

This paper highlights and explains the stance of various agencies within the U.S. Intelligence Community toward the adoption of succession management principles, which in turn aim to foster a more systematic approach to the development of future agency and Community leaders. This work thereby offers Community managers an inter-agency perspective from a neutral but well-informed point of view.

Proposed manuscripts for NDIC papers or books may be submitted to the Editor for consideration by the NDIC Press Editorial Board. Papers undergo review by senior officials in Defense, Intelligence and civilian academic or business communities. Manuscripts or requests for paper copies of papers or books should be addressed to Defense Intelligence Agency, National Defense Intelligence College, MC-X, Bolling AFB, Washington, DC 20340-5100.

ii | This publication has been approved for unrestricted distribution by the Office of Security Review, Department of Defense.

Russell G. Swenson, Editor in Chief
NDIC Press,
Russell.Swenson@dia.mil

CONTENTS

FOREWORD

During the years that I matriculated in the coursework associated with my doctoral program, one of my professors made a comment that was indelibly etched in my memory. The statement is so profound that I use it to gauge the change-supportiveness (or lack thereof) of leaders. Unbeknown to my professor, in his honor, I dubbed his comment "Diriker's Rule." Simply put, Dr. Diriker said, there are two mindsets that will kill any organization; they are: "One is that we've always done it that way, and the second is that we've never done it that way."

Unfortunately, "Diriker's Rule" is representative of the perspective from which many organizational leaders operate when it comes to succession management. From the position of "we've always done it that way," officials support succession management only as the identification of the next tier of individuals who will occupy leadership positions. In succession literature, this approach is labeled "replacement planning." It will not deliver the leadership pipeline that is consistent with the tenets of sustained organizational excellence.

"We've never done it that way," is the second aspect of "Diriker's Rule," and it gives insight into the change resistance of leadership. When it comes to succession management, officials' espousals of support are belied by their behavior. In other words, leaders say that they are interested in a broad-based, holistic approach to succession management. They say that they want to ensure the existence of an inclusive organizational culture; effective people-oriented systems and processes; and a collaborative, values-driven workplace. (All of the foregoing are components of an effective succession management process.) Yet, an examination of the "succession management" processes that currently are instituted in some organizations reveal either a complete lack of attention to this area, or a partial, ineffective response.

An effective succession management process is the lifeblood of an organization whose leadership is interested in long-term success. If you are such a leader, then I urge you to read this book. Beth Hatfield has authored a literary work that is a must-read for any individual who wants to ensure that the organization's approach to succession management is strategic and holistic; one that will perpetuate continuous organizational effectiveness. Ms. Hatfield delivers an insightful product that moves its readers beyond the use of replacement planning tools. While she focuses on the Intelligence Community, the lessons learned from this book are applicable to any leader regardless of whether he or she is a private or public sector leadership official. I am supportive of Ms. Hatfield's efforts, and I applaud her accomplished written work.

Debbie W. Ridley,

Intelligence Community

Organizational Scientist

ACKNOWLEDGMENTS

"It is hard to fail, but it is worse never to have tried to succeed."
— Theodore Roosevelt

There are so many who have contributed to this work, attempting to identify each person would ensure someone would be missed. However, my thanks go out first to each of the 21 interview participants. These senior Intelligence professionals graciously allowed me on their schedules, into their offices, and inside their thinking on succession management. Your earnest statements provide all that is worth reading in this book.

Also, my thanks go to the professionals in OPM's Strategic Human Resources Policy Division and Human Capital Leadership & Merit System Accountability Division. The insights regarding federal senior executives and OPM's work on succession provide the paper a welcome broad perspective. Current and past members of the Society of Competitive Intelligence Professionals (SCIP) reinforced the private sector perspective on intelligence executives and senior leader positions. The members of NSA's Senior Leadership Management Organization and NGA's Human Development Directorate offered a glimpse into their on-going succession work and the zeal with which they pursue it. Members of the Office of the Director of National Intelligence (ODNI) Senior Officer Management Office recommended improvements to the structure and readability of the paper. The faculty of NDIC, including career educators, retired military, and former federal executives, suggested avenues to investigate and fresh ideas to consider. Thank you all for your time and encouragement.

Ms. I. Rogers and SGM D. Hatfield, USA Retired, who kindly agreed to review the paper, deserve recognition for their expertise and contributions. These unselfish people had the lamentable task of reading the draft for information and analysis errors. You have my appreciation for your energy and enthusiasm.

My gratitude goes to the other Fellows and staff at the Center for Strategic Intelligence Research (CSIR). They should get bonuses for all the laughter and positive reinforcement. It will be hard to work without them.

Although the citations and analysis are my own work, any competent writing in this paper must be credited to Dr. R. Swenson, Director of the Center for Strategic Intelligence Research at the National Defense Intelligence College. Not only was he willing to take a chance on me as the first NSA Fellow in the CSIR program, he ensured the resulting product would be coherent, logical, and up to the standards of the Center and College. For that and for the many emails that made me laugh and kept me from leaping off ledges, my undying gratitude.

Finally—the best is always last—my husband, Dave, deserves some kind of plaque for putting up with all the whining, time spent on the computer (instead of on the Harley), and fast-food dinners. Thank you, Dr. Dave.

CHAPTER 1
Overture

Each year, the National Defense Intelligence College (NDIC) Center for Strategic Intelligence Research (CSIR) offers a group of national intelligence professionals the opportunity to advance the Intelligence Community's knowledge in specific areas of interest. Research Fellowships provide individuals from across the Intelligence Community (IC) a unique experience in conducting in-depth investigation into topics of personal and professional concern. The resulting publications broaden or deepen the Community leadership team's and employees' understanding of myriad topics. The experience also expands the Research Fellows' exposure to the Community, affords them the opportunity to focus exclusively on a single subject for six to twelve months, and allows them to publish their work. During the last year, the CSIR identified (human) resource management in the IC as a topic for research. The current paper on leader selection, development, and placement falls within this research theme.

Discovering Knowable Facts

History offers many examples of ways to choose leaders. It has been the last man standing after a duel, the eloquent visionary able to incite throngs of followers to action, or the person with the most votes after a popular election. Although sometimes difficult or resulting in unpalatable leaders, these selection methods are instantly recognizable. With senior IC officials unlikely to use duels, public oratory, or popular voting to select their replacements and other Community leaders, this paper explores how some of the IC agencies have been and are performing that task. What has been the method by which individuals were readied and chosen for positions of great authority and responsibility—how were and are our IC leaders being selected? And how should they be prepared and selected in the future? This paper suggests a plan for the implementation of succession management across the Community.

The Leader Issue

The 9/11 Commission found management of personnel to be one of the shortcomings of the Community in the wake of the devastating terrorist attacks.[1] The Commission Report holds that:

---

[1] *The 9/11 Commission Report: Final Report of the National Commission on Terrorist Attacks Upon the United States*, July 2004, 22-23.

A common set of personnel standards for intelligence can create a group of professionals better able to operate in joint activities, transcending their own service-specific mind-sets.[2]

OPM and IC surveys of the workforce focus attention on federal and Community leaders, respectively. In 2006, as part of its biennial query to federal employees, OPM gathered information on the workforce's perception of federal government leaders. In most areas evaluated, about one-half of federal employees hold positive views of their leaders. However, considerably fewer than half the employees judge that leaders have an ability to motivate the workforce.[3]

The Office of the Director of National Intelligence (ODNI) has conducted two employee climate surveys (in 2005 and 2006). To provide for comparison across the government, these surveys draw on the OPM survey format. The IC employees responded somewhat more positively about leaders than the combined federal workforce, but only by a small margin. For example, summary results indicate that IC employees are happier with their leaders than are federal government employees at large by a margin of less than 5%.[4] Both surveys highlight a disturbing unease with the caliber of leaders.

Given these concerns and the mission of the DNI to bring more cohesiveness to the IC, an obligation exists to improve the process of identifying, preparing, and placing leaders across the IC. DNI McConnell's 100-Day Plan does see personnel management as a priority activity.[5] The term *succession* appears several times in the DNI's five-year human capital plan for the IC.[6]

> **"**
> **How can the DNI advance the IC toward implementing succession management?**
> **"**

For the near term, most IC leaders will likely be drawn from the current senior executive corps. However, if past assessments of the federal Senior Executive Service (SES) corps are accurate and representative of the intelli-

---

2 *The 9/11 Commission Report: Final Report of the National Commission on Terrorist Attacks Upon the United States,* 409.

3 All the results, trend analysis, and demographic information about the Federal Human Capital Survey 2006 conducted by OPM may be found on-line at *http://www.fhcs2006.opm.gov.*

4 Office of the Director of National Intelligence, *IC Annual Employee Climate Survey: IC Survey 2006, Survey Results* (Office of the Intelligence Community Chief Human Capital Officer (CHCO): March 2007), attachment to e-mail from Stephen J. Kerda, Member NDIC Staff, to NDIC Staff (alias), 19 April 2007.

5 Michael McConnell, Office of the Director of National Intelligence, *United States Intelligence Community (IC): 100 Day Plan for Integration and Collaboration,* 2007.

6 *The U.S. Intelligence Community's Five Year Strategic Human Capital Plan* (Office of the Director of National Intelligence, 2006), 14, 36, 39.

gence Senior Executives subset, these individuals are neither fungible across intelligence organizations, nor prepared for the net-centric environment of today, much less for other looming challenges.[7] Some may be hired from the private sector, but with the discouraging rate of success for those hired from outside an organization,[8] most will have to be developed within the IC.

In these circumstances, how do we grow individuals who can lead? What kind of plan can develop, place, and continually refresh technically respected, managerially strong intelligence leaders, who take for granted an integrated, thoroughly networked Community? Based on Congressional and workforce concerns about the quantity and quality of senior leaders now and in the future, this paper explores the internal preparation and selection of future leaders for the IC through the question: *How can the DNI advance the IC toward implementing succession management?*

To answer this question, the paper mines the literature and reviews federal statutes and regulations on senior executive management to delineate what can be done to support a change in managing the Community's leaders. Interviews with IC experts illuminate current perspectives on succession management, identifying areas of agreement and dissonance between agencies (see Interview Questions). In the end, the findings will lay out reasonable actions to be taken in preparation for developing and implementing succession management across the IC.

7 Donald F. Kettl, and others, *Civil Service Reform: Building a Government That Works* (Washington, DC: Brookings Institution Press, 1996), 55-57.

8 In their article, "Passing the Torch of Leadership," in *Leader to Leader* (Spring 2006, 37-44), Robert Gandossy and Nidhi Verma indicate that internally selected CEOs perform better than externally recruited CEOs; they assert that external hiring also sends a negative message to the internal workforce. Additionally, James Walker, in asking "Do We Need Succession Planning Anymore" (*Human Resource Planning*, Vol 21, 9+, 1998) responds that we do; he suggests that external hires may have assimilation issues, including working with the extant leadership team.

1. History and current process

   a. How has your organization/agency approached top-echelon succession management (top three levels of senior executive leaders, but below the level of political appointees) over the last five years? How is it done now?

   b. Who/what organization is the lead for succession management?

   c. What tools are used to gather data for succession planning/modeling?

2. Agency culture

   a. What is the focus of your agency's documented workforce management strategy? How does it link to the agency's mission?

   b. What are the management trends or philosophies embraced by your agency?

   c. How could your agency improve its approach to succession management?

3. External factors

   a. What is your agency's participation in the various boards associated with workforce and/or executive succession management?

   b. With what private sector succession management plans and achievements are you familiar?

   c. What do you see as the external factors affecting succession management for your agency?

Interview Questions. *Source: Author.*

Useful Terms

This paper rests on consistent definitions of leaders and succession management. The following definitions apply throughout the paper.

Succession management is "a structured effort by an organization to ensure continuity in key positions and to retain and develop intellectual and knowledge capital for the future."[9] The terms succession management, succession planning, succession process, and talent management appear interchangeably in this paper.

---

[9] *A Guide to Succession Management* (Nova Scotia, Canada: Nova Scotia Public Service Commission, 2005), Link from URL: *http://www.gov.ns.ca/pac/*, accessed 16 August 2006, 4.

Leader (or leadership) refers to the top three tiers of career, civilian intelligence Senior Executives within each named IC agency, but below the level of political appointee. IC leaders, then, comprise the top three tiers of civilians who provide continuity between the workforce and successive appointed officials (generally, agency Directors); they ensure some stability in the long-term execution of each member agency's and the IC's mission(s). Therefore, those discussed here as leaders may be the Deputy Director, the Chief of Staff, and Director/Chief of a large, subordinate organization, or those reporting directly to them. Example positions for each tier are provided in Chapter Three.

Qualitative analysis, as applied in this paper, requires that the investigation result in certified evaluative criteria for better understanding of the "subject set."[10] Rather than measuring phenomena related to the topic to confirm or refute hypotheses, the researcher uses questions to develop the evaluative criteria. This approach ensures that the work can be extended by other investigators. The ultimate value of this study will lie in the application of knowledge gained. The actions and evaluative criteria should facilitate knowledge application by IC staff and be of value to the Community's employees at large.

Beyond The Margin

Academics sometimes observe a distinction between leaders and managers (or administrators). Though fascinating, that debate rages elsewhere, not in this paper. Rather than join that discussion, this paper assumes that skills to both manage and lead are required at the highest levels in the IC. Therefore, for this paper, the two terms remain interchangeable.

Whatever one may think of succession management in the U.S. Armed Forces, the path of preparation and selection for advancement is clear, certainly for those in uniform. However, civilians within the Services may offer a different perspective on preparation and promotion opportunities. Although insights into each Service's civilian succession management may prove interesting, this paper focuses only on the IC civilians in Community agencies.

The IC has continued to expand since its inception. Rather than attempt to consider all IC organizations, in this paper, the spotlight falls on the larger, independent agencies in the IC: Central Intelligence Agency (CIA), Defense Intelligence Agency (DIA), National Geospatial-Intelligence Agency (NGA), National Reconnaissance Organization (NRO), and the National Security

---

10 Carl F. Auerback and Louise B. Silverstein, *Qualitative Data: An Introduction to Coding and Analysis* (New York, New York University Press, 2003), 4-6.

Agency (NSA). To provide the collective, Community perspective, the Under Secretary of Defense (Intelligence) (USD(I)) and ODNI were also included. Intelligence organizations operating within larger establishments, such as the Bureau of Intelligence and Research (INR) within the State Department, remain a subject for a different study.

CHAPTER 2
The Process

It is impossible to reduce natural leadership to a set of skills or competencies. Ultimately, people follow people who believe in something and have the abilities to achieve results in the service of those beliefs. [11]

From a programmatic view, any process for developing or acquiring a resource must include clearly articulated requirements. This is no less true for a program to identify and prepare IC leaders. To define what we mean by *leader* in the IC, this chapter reviews academic and popular literature about leaders: their cognitive abilities, behaviors, and operating environments. In addition, the chapter reviews much of the literature on succession management. Taken together, these elements promote the IC's interest in developing a defensible plan to grow intelligence leaders.

Defining The Leader Requirement

The study of leaders and leadership spans millennia. The ancient Greeks sought to understand the defining qualities of leaders. The great thinkers of the Middle Ages and Renaissance attempted to describe the mindset and actions of leaders. During the Industrial Revolution, observers tried to document the mechanics performed by effective workers and managers. As the twentieth century progressed, academicians undertook efforts to quantify the nature of good leadership, thus providing evidence of what constitutes a good leader. Leaders themselves have offered views of their own strengths and shortcomings in autobiographies and monographs on leadership and being a leader.[12] Yet, there appear to be no conclusions about what defines the ideal leader and how to identify him or her with absolute certainty. Regardless, the continued research and popular culture analysis of leadership and leaders emphasizes the critical need for these elusive individuals. The aim here is to clarify the relevancy of selected literature for application in IC succession management.

---

11 Peter M. Senge, *The Fifth Discipline: The Art & Practice of the Learning Organization* (New York: Currency Doubleday, 1990), 360.

12 Thomas J. Wren, *The Leader's Companion: Insights on Leadership through the Ages* (New York: The Free Press, 1995).

"Great man" theories suggest that all great leaders possess innate abilities beyond those of the masses or that heroes step forward when needed. These born leaders seem destined for greatness. Although these conceptions appear to have fallen out of favor, some theories do suggest that traits common to "good" leaders can be identified. Bennis identifies recurring traits found in leaders he interviewed: continual learning, risk taking, reflection (on one's life and experiences), and "mastery of the task at hand." [13]

The Heroic Leader General George Washington, "First in War, first in Peace and first in the hearts of his countrymen." *Source: Agence France Press.*

In his book, *Leadership*, James MacGregor Burns distinguishes two leader types: the hero (worshiped by followers) and the administrator (manages activities and resources). Ultimately, he advocates the ideal of having in place an inspsirational leader who influences his followers to undertake their own betterment, as part of the process of achieving shared goals. This "transforming" leadership is a continuing process whereby the leader learns about the motivations and needs of followers and through introspection determines his own motivations and needs.[14] Kouzes and Posner reiterate that leadership represents "a relationship between those who aspire to lead and those who choose to follow."[15] The leader must not only communicate the goals to followers, she must exemplify the behavior desired in reaching those goals. From their research, Kouzes and Posner cite four leader characteristics as the top responses from those surveyed, regardless of country or culture: leaders should be honest, forward-looking, competent, and inspiring.[16] One can hardly argue against any of these leader characteristics—no one wants

---

[13] Warren Bennis, *On Becoming a Leader* (Reading, MA: Addison-Wesley Publishing Company, 1989), 9.

[14] James MacGregor Burns, *Leadership* (New York: Harper & Row, 1978), 460.

[15] James M. Kouzes and Barry Z. Posner, *The Leadership Challenge*, 3rd rev. ed. (San Francisco, CA: Jossey-Bass, 2002), 20.

[16] Kouzes and Posner, 25.

a dishonest or incapable leader. So the issues appear to be what general and IC-specific characteristics will be valued and needed in the future and what mechanisms will be used to identify them efficiently in individuals.

In addition to these characteristics, IC succession planners can consider what traits might be required for success in the context of the positions future leaders will hold. The work of Stephen Zaccaro on executive models of leadership is helpful when considering the increasingly intricate situations faced by senior leaders. Zaccaro observes that "The premise of the theories and models [on *conceptual complexity*] is that the working or operating environment of senior organizational leaders is of such complexity that leader success becomes predicated on the possession and application of higher order cognitive abilities and skills."[17] Jacobs and McGee consider conceptual complexity "of unusual significance in the determination of success and failure in the rarified atmosphere found at the strategic apex of large-scale organizations." [18] For example, as the Community faces technological challenges, we should expect our leaders not only to understand the technical jargon of the day, but to have mastered the conceptual complexities at play and be able to communicate with the workforce in understandable terms the mission impact of those complexities.

The Inspirational Leader Mahatma Gandhi. *Source: Agence France Press.*

> "
> This "transforming" leadership is a continuing process whereby the leader learns about the motivations and needs of followers and through introspection determines his own motivations and needs.
> "

Behavior complexity theory is based on what the leader does—as demonstrated in responses to the variety of activities in which the leader

| 9

17 Stephen J. Zaccaro, *Models and Theories of Executive Leadership: A Conceptual/Empirical Review and Integration* (U.S. Army Research Institute for the Behavioral and Social Sciences, 1996), 25.

18 Stephen J. Zaccaro and Richard J. Klimoski, eds., *The Nature of Organizational Leadership: Understanding the Performance Imperatives Confronting Today's Leaders, The Organizational Frontiers* (San Francisco: Jossey-Bass, 2001), 74.

engages.[19] Zaccaro cites Hooijberg and Schneider's suggestion that "leaders who are high in behavioral complexity and social intelligence will be more effective in developing informed foresight, co-opting internal and external stakeholders, and viewing the organization within its larger social system."[20] Other aspects of behavioral theories consider the symbiotic nature of the leader-subordinate relationship. Each affects the other through stimulus-response. For example, the leader may incentivize the subordinate with a reward for an increased output; the subordinate, in return, reacts with a positive attitude and continued performance, thus encouraging continued positive reinforcement from the leader. The basics of conceptual and behavioral complexity theories are outlined below.

Conceptual	Behavioral
• Establish framework for the mission	• Affect subordinate behavior achieving through actions
• Plan for increasingly lengthy timelines	• Are influenced by subordinate responses
• Requires mental flexibility and organizational knowledge	• Play multiple roles within and across the organization
• Developed through assignments & mentoring	• Developed through training and assignments to learn new behavior strategies
Source: Zaccaro, *Models and Theories of Executive Leadership: A Conceptual/ Empirical Review and Integration*, 354.	Sources: Zaccaro, 354; Bass, *Bass and Stogdill's Handbook of Leadership: Theory, Research and Managerial Applications*, 48-49.

Conceptual and Behavioral Complexity Models. *Source: Author.*

Stratified systems theory describes an organization in which the leader must convey the intent of those at the higher levels in the structure to those at the lower levels; the leader, then, must understand his superiors' strategic intent and communicate that in terms of the subordinates' tactical actions to be taken. As the leader moves into the higher levels of the organization, the

---

19 Stephen J. Zaccaro, *The Nature of Executive Leadership: A Conceptual and Empirical Analysis of Success* (Washington, DC: American Psychological Association, 2001), 17

20 Zaccaro and Klimoski, eds., *The Nature of Organizational Leadership*, 125.

environment becomes more focused on the long-term and ambiguous.[21] The leader becomes the interpreter or intermediary between levels in the organization. The Table "Other Leadership Models" distills additional aspects of leadership that emerge from two other models.

Perspectives	Focus of Executive Leadership	Executive Performance Requirements	Changes in Performance Requirements in Ascending Organizational Levels	Requisite Executive Characteristics	Developmental Prescription
Strategic Decision-making Models	To create and manage a co-alignment between organizational elements and environment characteristics, through the development of a long-term strategy	Environment and organization scanning, information interpretation and sense-making, strategy formation and implementation	No clear difference articulated; however, executive leaders are more likely to be responsible for strategy formation, while more junior leaders are more likely to be responsible for day-to-day strategy implementation	Cognitive abilities, knowledge of operating environmental and functional expertise, need for achievement, locus of control, self-efficacy, risk propensity, flexibility	No clear prescriptions offered; the importance of functional expertise in this framework suggests that potential executives should be provided with work opportunities in many functional domains within the organization
Inspirational/Visionary Leadership Models	To change and manage organizational processes in line with an articulated vision; to inspire, motivate, and empower subordinates so that they share responsibility for organizational change	Charismatic or idealized influence on subordinates; providing inspirational motivation, intellectual stimulation, and individualized consideration to subordinates	No differences articulated; transformational leadership can occur at all organizational levels. However, some models suggest that guiding organizational visions are more likely to be articulated by executive leaders.	Cognitive abilities, self-confidence, socialized power motives, social skills, nurturance skills, risk propensity	Potential executives should be provided with opportunities for self-understanding regarding their own leadership styles, and training to learn both transformational and transactional leadership behaviors

Other Leadership Models.[22] *Source: Author.*

---

21 Bernard M. Bass, *Bass and Stogdill's Handbook of Leadership: Theory, Research, and Managerial Applications*, 3rd ed. (New York: The Free Press, 1990), 51-52.

22 Zaccaro, *Models and Theories of Executive Leadership*, 354.

As these diverse models show, no single definition of leader or leadership exists. Theories, the number of which continues to grow, offer a stunning breadth and depth of information upon which IC succession planners may draw. More than food for thought, the theories' suggestions can be used in crafting the specifications or competencies for senior leaders, including their required experiences, and the positions we expect them to hold. For example, the capacity to understand and operate in a complex environment may be linked to a position in which the leader has responsibility for initiating or continuing transformation efforts. It may seem easier to start and stay with the current IC definitions of *leader* (whatever they may be), but academic work may provide depth and gravity to our understanding of what we *really* need from our future leaders.

Although the desirability of succession management for the IC remains one of the present paper's assumptions, for completeness the next section draws on the literature to make the case for implementing succession. Next, some of the indicators of an environment primed for success are pulled from the literature. The literature exploration ends with a depiction of potential sources of resistance to succession management.

Succession Concepts

Googling the Web in search of information on leaders, leadership, and succession management is like drinking from a fire hose. Barbara Kellerman, a faculty member at the Center for Public Leadership at the Kennedy School, mentions the popularity of leader and leadership as a topic for higher learning institutions and for commercial endeavors. She rightly refers to this continuously growing group as the *leadership industry*.[23] However, some organizations distinguish themselves from the crowded field through their contributions to leader development and succession, their membership, or their client list.

For example, the Corporate Leadership Council's Corporate Executive Board offers research to its members on a variety of management tools and practices, including succession management. The Center for Creative Leadership, a non-profit organization, offers development opportunities for current and future leaders. Other organizations, such as the National Academy of Public Administration (chartered by Congress to aid local, state, and federal governments with management effectiveness) and RAND (a non-profit research and analysis organization), research and report on a wide range of administration and personnel topics such as succession and development.

---

23 Barbara Kellerman, *Bad Leadership: What It Is, How It Happens, Why It Matters* (Boston, MA: Harvard Business School Press, 2004), 3.

Individuals often cited within the field include William Rothwell (consultant and Professor of Human Resource Development at The Pennsylvania State University) and Stewart Friedman (Practice Professor of Management at the Wharton School of The University of Pennsylvania). Combining the academic sources and for-profit organizations, the list of those offering information or assistance on succession management appears unlimited.

With work being done on the topic of succession by such a large field, it should come as no surprise that much as the definition of leader varies from one source to another so does the concept of succession. *Replacement planning*, one of the commonly used alternative terms, refers to the identification of individuals to assume the jobs of departing leaders. Often done as the organization struggles with an unexpected departure such as a dismissal or death, this crisis response approach to managing leaders bears little resemblance to a process of preparing and placing the best and brightest in the organization's most critical positions. The literature, in referring to an approach that anticipates departures, particularly of senior-most leaders, employs the terms *succession planning* and *succession management*, often interchangeably. Some articles and a few subjects interviewed for this paper add the phrase *talent management* in describing a recruiting-to-retiring lifecycle of preparing and positioning high-quality individuals in the workforce, particularly as leaders.

The present paper uses the term *succession management* to describe "a structured effort by an organization to ensure continuity in key positions and retain and develop intellectual and knowledge capital for the future."[24] This term goes beyond the traditional one-for-one replacement of senior leaders to address the organization's long-term leader needs. It was with this definition in mind that succession literature was reviewed.

> There is no more important human capital issue confronting the federal government than the methods and systems for selecting, developing, and managing its executive leaders. [25]

---

24 *A Guide to Succession Management*, 4.

25 Patricia W. Ingraham and others, Strengthening Senior Leadership in the U.S. Government in Phase I Report (Washington, DC: National Academy of Public Administration, 2000), URL: <http://www.napawash.org/publications.html,> accessed 11 July 2006., v.

Why Do It

The literature suggests some consensus on the need for succession, but the rationale for it varies. The most significant and often-cited justification is the continued graying of the workforce.[26] For both the private and public sectors, the anticipated departure of the large baby-boomer population appears as an impending crisis. This generation, born between 1946 and 1964, made available some 80 million people to the workforce. In testimony before Congress in 2001, the Government Accountability Office (GAO) indicated that 58% of the Defense Department workforce would be eligible for retirement by 2006.[27] Although baby-boomer departures to date appear to be fewer than projected,[28] it is only a matter of time before the departures are upon us.

Not only will these knowledgeable individuals be departing, but they are followed by a significantly smaller workforce from which to draft their replacements—Generation X (born 1965-1981, approximately 46 million people).[29] To prepare IC organizations for the wave of departures and ensure that sufficient replacements exist, a process should be in place to define or redefine the work that must be done. This process includes prioritization of activities, allowing for a redistribution of tasks to a smaller number or reconfigured organization of senior leaders. Additionally, such work may indicate circumstances for the rehiring or retention of baby-boomers for knowledge transfer or short-term transition.

A second rationale for implementing succession management highlights the need to select quality individuals to lead. Whatever the procedures, the identification of the most promising future leaders, often referred to as high potentials (or *hipos*), should not be left to happenstance.[30] Having in place a system—a coordinated body of methods or a complex scheme or plan of procedures, such as a system of organization and management; or any reg-

---

26 Lynne C. Lancaster and David Stillman, "If I Pass the Baton, Who Will Grab It? Creating Bench Strength in Public Management," *Public Management*, September 2005.

27 U.S. Congress, Joint Hearings, *Subcommittee on Oversight of Government Management, Restructuring and the District of Columbia, Committee on Governmental Affairs, Senate, and Subcommittee on Civil Service and Agency Organization, Committee on Government Reform, House, Human Capital: Major Human Capital Challenges at the Departments of Defense and State,* Hearings, 107th Cong., 1st sess., 29 March 2001, 8.

28 Sources, Senior-Level Personnel at OPM, who wish to remain anonymous, interview by author, 31 January 2007.

29 Lancaster and Stillman.

30 Thomas S. McFee and others, *Leadership for Leaders: Senior Executives and Middle Managers*, August 2003, 5.

ular or special method of plan or procedures[31] —increases confidence that the best and brightest will be prepared and placed to achieve success.

Succession management:
- Scopes the work of tomorrow
- Identifies and systematically prepares future leaders to respond to the Baby Boomer departures
- Supports continued organizational health
- Assures smooth leader transitions
- Continues to address corporate issues

Making the Case. *Source: Author.*

This seems counterintuitive to the traditional notion of "cream rising to the top." However, if, as Bennis suggests, short-term success is sometimes more valued by selection officials than long-term achievement, none but those satisfying the immediate goals will be chosen as leaders without an institutionalized system of selection.[32] In light of the information on impending talent shortages, this process to select and ready future leaders takes on even greater importance. Without such preparation, the result could be, as reported by the Corporate Leadership Council, "an ever-younger, less-seasoned executive bench and the possibility of promotion of managers with significant gaps in their development."[33]

From small, family-owned companies to multi-national corporations, one must assume the imperative of continuing the business; this is the responsibility, and ensures the legacy, of departing leaders.[34] For the IC, that assumption means that the production of intelligence for consumers must continue unaffected by leader changes. At stake for the Community is the availability of leaders who can continue to garner support (resources) for making necessary advances in technology and personnel to best serve consumers. An additional challenge will be to place leaders willing and able to continue the change and transformation efforts undertaken by today's IC leaders.

Third, without guidelines in place to help, filling the shoes of departing employees can be difficult, both in terms of finding the needed talent and

---

31 Benjamin S. Blanchard and Wolter J. Fabrycky, *Systems Engineering and Analysis*, 2nd ed. (Englewood Cliffs, NJ: Prentice Hall, 1990), 1-2.

32 Bennis, 8.

33 Corporate Leadership Council-Corporate Executive Board, *The Next Generation: Accelerating the Development of Rising Leaders*, Report, 1997, 13.

34 Roz Ayres-Williams, "Making Sure You Go the Distance: Show You've Planned for the Long Haul by Having a Succession Plan in Place," *Black Enterprise*, April 1998.

reducing the length of time positions remain vacant. The impact of not having a process in place can be seen in other ways, as well. For example, during the confirmation hearings for Vice Admiral McConnell (USN, Retired) for the position of DNI, Senators could be heard on C-SPAN expressing concern about the long-vacant position of Deputy DNI—unfilled since May 2006, when the departing Deputy DNI, General Hayden, USAF, took over as Director of CIA. Vice Admiral McConnell was questioned on his sense of urgency to select a deputy. This situation—a critical position remaining unfilled for an extended period of time—occurs at all levels in both public- and private-sector organizations. Succession management offers the mechanism for quickly validating the requirements of critical jobs. Further, by anticipating departures, it allows a smooth transition of authority to those ready, willing, and able to take control of an organization.[35] Minimizing the turbulence caused by the expected exodus of the baby boomers will be a challenge. Effective succession management enables employees at all levels to prepare for that transition.

Finally, Rothwell suggests succession management as a means for dealing with critical corporate issues such as diversity.[36] In laying out the organization's succession management priorities, diversity can be highlighted as a significant consideration in and outcome of the process.[37] In its final report on a two-year study of the 21st century federal manager, the National Academy of Public Administration (NAPA) suggests succession as a way to achieve diversity in managers or leaders at all levels of an organization by considering the departures of senior and mid-level managers not as a threat, but an opportunity. Vacancies offer Community selection officials the chance to vary the backgrounds represented on the leadership team. Adding emphasis to diversity in the process of identifying and preparing future IC leaders increases the likelihood of a leadership team that reflects the intelligence consumer and U.S. population demographics.[38]

Focusing on the benefits of succession management, IC succession planners should be able to make a reasonable case for implementation. There may still be resistance to such a change, but those throwing up roadblocks may find it difficult to argue plausibly against a process by which the right

---

35 Christine Smith, "Eagan Minnesota: Growth with Grace," *Public Management,* December 2005.

36 William J. Rothwell, PhD, SPH, *Effective Succession Planning,* 3rd ed. (New York: American Management Association (AMACOM), 2005), 19.

37 Michael Leibman and others, "Succession Management: The Next Generation of Succession Planning," *Human Resource Planning* 19, no. 3 (1996): 16+.

38 Thomas S. McFee and others, *Final Report and Recommendations: The 21st Century Federal Manager,* Final Report of *The 21st Century Federal Manager Series,* February 2004, 38-39.

people are prepared and placed in positions closely, if not ideally, suited to their skills, knowledge, and ability.

Achievement Takes More than Luck

Although the professional literature presents often divergent recommendations for implementing succession, agreement does exist on some basics. Most significant among these is the involvement and commitment of an organization's senior leader, the CEO (for private-sector organizations) or the Director (for IC organizations). The specifics of this involvement depend upon the procedures put in place. However, a consensus exists that senior leaders must be engaged in the creation or validation of the vision for succession management,[39] use of the process to select senior leaders,[40] and oversight of its implementation.[41] Some suggest that senior leaders be active in mentoring and coaching future successors.[42] Finally, ensuring that appropriate resources are allocated to the effort is another responsibility of senior leaders; providing the staff and budget for initiating and maintaining succession demonstrates leaders' commitment to the effort.[43]

Frequently, the literature affirms the value of involving human resource (HR) or human capital (HC) management at the outset of any implementation of succession management. As organizations still unfamiliar with a disciplined approach to leader development and selection attempt to implement succession management, human resource/capital managers may be called on to inform the leadership team about how to begin. By drawing on internal and, perhaps, external expertise, the HR/HC organization acts as a senior advisor and educator for the senior leaders.[44] Succession management relies on or is integrated with a number of traditional HR/HC functions such as evaluation, promotion and rewards, and personnel data management. Based on this interdependence, the senior leadership team benefits from having HR/HC representation in the succession discussions—both to bring knowledge of current processes and to provide the data upon which decisions may

---

39 Thomas G. Gutteridge and others, "A New Look at Organizational Career Development," *Human Resource Planning* 16, no. 2 (1993): 71+.

40 Richard Donkin, "Time to Pay Attention to Management Succession," *The Financial Times*, 15 September 2005, 15.

41 U.S. Congress, House, Subcommittee on Civil Service and Agency Reorganization, Committee on House Government Reform, *Improving Productivity of Federal Workforce*, Hearings, 108th Cong., 1st sess., 1 October 2003.

42 Corporate Leadership Council-Corporate Executive Board, 275.

43 Steward D. Friedman, "Succession Systems in Large Corporations," in *Leadership Succession*, ed. Steward D. Friedman (New Brunswick, NJ: Transaction Books, 1986), 17.

44 James W. Walker and James M. LaRocco, "Succession Management and the Board," *Corporate Board*, Jan-Feb 2004, 10-16.

be made.[45] Whether recommending that the HR or HC organization engage in educating and directly advising senior leaders or adopt a more supportive role in "aligning" other processes with succession, research suggests the value inherent in intense participation by HR/HC personnel.

The adage that patience is a virtue may be no truer than when applied to implementation of succession management. The successive processes of implementing and seeing a return on investment from succession management are both long-term issues.[46] Senior leaders and the workforce should be committed to allowing the process to mature over time—not expecting immediate gratification.[47] For the private sector, breaking into new markets or expanding the customer list takes time and dedication, just as transforming the IC culture has taken (and continues to take) time. Developing an individual employee's capabilities should be viewed as an equally worthwhile and continuing effort.[48] In assessing NRO's Succession Management Program against industry best practices, the Personnel Decisions Research Institutes suggested that implementing succession management should be viewed as a multi-year effort, adding at least one year for each tier (grade or level) brought into the process.[49] This idea of succession as an enduring effort appears frequently in the literature. "Systematic leadership development is a strategic choice, representing a long-term investment in an organization's future and that of its employees."[50]

- Supportive and participative senior leaders
- Involved HR/HC organization
- Patience with the process
- Strong links to enterprise business strategy and requirements

---

Success Factors. *Source: Author.*

---

[45] Leibman and others, 16+.

[46] Ingraham and others, *Strengthening Senior Leadership in the U.S. Government.*

[47] Anita Dennis, "Succession-Planning Dos and Don'ts: Who Will Take over When You're Ready to Retire? If You Don't Know, It's Time to Decide," *Journal of Accountancy* 199, no. 2 (2005): 47+.

[48] "Effective Succession Management," *Personnel Today*, 19 November 2002, 4.

[49] Eleanor M. Smith and others, *A Preliminary Evaluation of the NRO Succession Management Program*, Technical Report 477 (Arlington, VA: Personnel Decisions Research Institutes, Inc., September 2004), 26.

[50] Robert Pernick, "Creating a Leadership Development Program: Nine Essential Tasks," *Public Management*, August 2002, 10+.

Finally, succession management must be tightly coupled with the organization's long-term business or mission strategy. Considering the operational needs of the organization in terms of its strategic plan is one of the first steps in defining a succession management plan. The results of this work form the foundation for specifying the needed skills and attributes of future leaders against which candidates will be assessed.[51] This work cannot be taken lightly, as it ties together the organization's future with the development of its future leaders.[52] It may also identify those unique skills which can be more readily acquired through outside hiring. As organizations consider future budgets and long-term technical or mission issues, succession planners fold the results of these discussions into their plans. For IC succession planners, Community peer groups can be founts of useful information in ensuring that the issue of strategic leadership is accounted for in the process of creating the Community's vision.

Government organizations have already acknowledged the critical link between an organization's strategic needs and its leader needs. In its 2005 review of succession efforts at the Census Bureau, the Department of Labor (DOL), the Veteran's Health Administration (VHA), and the Environmental Protection Agency (EPA), the Government Accountability Office highlighted the importance of linking succession to strategic planning. GAO indicated that this measure moves the organization toward meeting future rather than current needs.[53] It reinforces much of the literature in defining succession as an integrated process—not a stand-alone task.

---

51 Roselinde Torres and William Pasmore, "How to Successfully Manage CEO Succession," *Corporate Board* 26, no. 152 (2005): 8.

52 *Human Capital: Selected Agencies Have Opportunities to Enhance Existing Succession Planning and Management Efforts*, pg 13.

53 *Human Capital: Selected Agencies Have Opportunities to Enhance Existing Succession Planning and Management Efforts*, 2005, GAO-05-585, 13.

Mechanics

The figure below illustrates the five major components of succession management, as suggested by the literature.

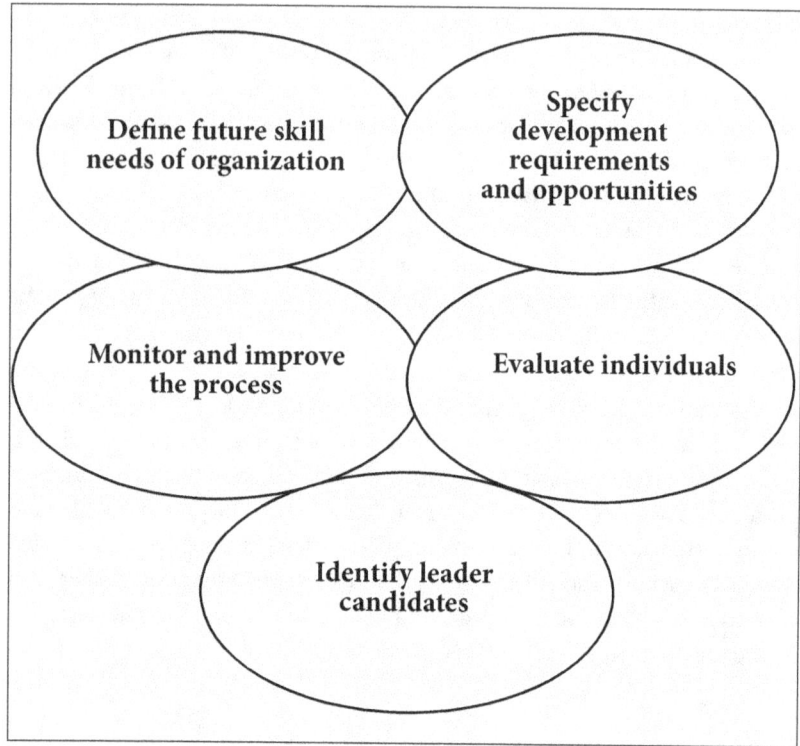

Pieces of the Process. *Source: Author.*

By building on the statement of leader requirements (the succession management needs statement), organizations may be better able to identify development opportunities for future leaders. Agreement among those who have explored this area is overwhelming. Observers agree that several methods of development are essential: classroom training, assignments, mentoring, and self-development. [54]

The Intelligence Community maintains several educational and training institutions, the Joint Military Intelligence Training Center (JMITC), the National Cryptologic School (NCS), The Kent School, and the National Geo-

---

[54] Ralph Bledsoe and others, *Building Successful Organizations: A Guide to Strategic Workforce Planning* (Washington, DC: National Academy of Public Administration Center for Human Resources Management, 2000), link from URL: <http://www.napawash.org/publications. html>, accessed 11 July 2006.

spatial-Intelligence Agency College, for example. These and related, online training opportunities offer IC professionals ample opportunity to participate in learning. The succession literature suggests classroom and on-line training have their place in developing future leaders; however, the effectiveness of this training rests on its application[55] in the workplace.

A report by the Corporate Leadership Council identified rotational assignments as a best practice in private-sector organizations having succession management in place. These seem most helpful in stretching candidates if they provide experience in new divisions within the organization and have a documented and widely understood purpose.[56] A 2004 RAND study of General and Flag Officers reviewed the required rotational assignments for this cadre and attempted to identify appropriate assignment and development patterns. In doing so, RAND categorized positions into jobs for growth and jobs for application. The conclusions address the length of each type of position, the balance of risk to the organization (in the event of failure) against the development potential for the assigned individuals, the importance of communication to the success of rotational assignments, and the critical role of senior leaders.[57] For IC succession planners, it may not be enough to have organizations simply identify potential assignments; establishing a procedure for managing the long-term implications for the individual (ensuring that the skills specified for an assignment are acquired) and the organization (ensuring quality output from the rotated candidates) may be required for success.

> The key aspect of this study is the distinction between what we call "developing" jobs and "using" jobs. This distinction rests on the principle that work experience accumulates through a variety of manager and executive assignments that prepare the individual for increasingly demanding and complex jobs. Early assignments build functional skills, organizational knowledge, and personal insights. Later jobs tend to have more complex and ambiguous responsibilities that draw on skills and knowledge developed in earlier assignments.[58]

Excerpt from RAND Study.

---

55 Paul Bernthal and Richard Wellins, "Trends in Leader Development and Succession," *Human Resource Planning* 29, no. 2 (2006): 31+.

56 Corporate Leadership Council-Corporate Executive Board, *The Next Generation: Accelerating the Development of Rising Leaders,* 33.

57 Margaret C. Harrell and others, *Aligning the Stars: Improvements to General and Flag Officer Management* (Santa Monica, CA: RAND, 2004), 20 and 54-56.

58 Harrell and others, *Aligning the Stars: Improvements to General and Flag Officer Management,* xvi-xvii.

Aligning the Stars: Improvements to General and Flag Officer Management

Mentoring provides guidance from seniors in the organization who offer a candidate the strategic view of issues facing the organization, an important aspect of developing future leaders. Some of the literature refers to mentors as those providing candidates a safe environment in which to question themselves, helping them define their developmental needs.[59] Other writers suggest the mentor helps the candidate map out career plans and may even exert influence on behalf of the candidate.[60] In any case, the relationship provides the candidate support for learning about the organization and navigating the advancement rapids.

Finally, self-development seems so critical that it has been cited as an indicator of potential in individuals.[61] A number of publications suggest that self-assessment and improvement are required of those who are or will be leaders.[62] Kouzes and Posner declare, "In the end, we realize that leadership development is ultimately self-development."[63]

Evaluating individuals as a function of the succession process is another area where experts have independently reached agreement. This concept has two meanings—both evaluation of current performance and evaluation of potential. The first and obvious purpose is to determine that the mission of the organization is being realized through evaluation of the individual's performance in terms of present requirements. Not only does this permit an identification of the top performers, but the evaluation itself reveals what the organization considers to be important.[64] IC succession planners may determine collaboration to be the most effective means for establishing consistency (or at least compatibility) in the various evaluation, compensation, and recognition methods used across the Community. Particularly as people increasingly move from one organization to another, confidence that the best and brightest are being exchanged will be critical. Trust in the evaluation mechanisms of other organizations provides that foundation.

---

59 McFee and others, *Final Report and Recommendations: The 21st Century Federal Manager*, 53-54.

60 Billie G. Blair, "Nothing Succeeds Like Succession Planning," Security Management, September 2005.

61 Lynn Miller, "Initiative for Self-Development Identifies Future Leaders," HRMagazine, January 2001, 20.

62 Deborah G. Barger, *Toward a Revolution in Intelligence Affairs*, A RAND Report (Washington, DC: 2005), 68.

63 Kouzes and Posner, xxviii.

64 Edgar H. Schein, *Organizational Culture and Leadership* (San Francisco, CA: Jossey-Bass Publishers, 1985), 79.

The second category of evaluation is that used to determine potential, which is critical to identifying future leaders.[65] Evaluation tools suggested include the 360° assessment, interviews, and talent centers.[66] Note that most of the literature refers to the placement of these candidate leaders in *pools*. One of the arguments for identifying candidate leaders, whether or not pools are created, rests on the ability to focus limited resources on those assessed to be the most likely to succeed. However, development resources should be available to pools of future leaders at *all* levels in the organization, not just those waiting to ascend to the executive level.[67] Availability of developmental opportunities for leaders at all levels ensures depth in the organization's leader bench strength, an approach recommended by much of the succession literature.

> **Development resources should be available to pools of future leaders at all levels in the organization, not just those waiting to ascend to the executive level.**

In evaluation and selection of candidates, IC succession planners should be aware that it may be difficult to identify individuals with potential early in their careers; establishing pools may be a mitigation strategy for this, allowing fluidity to the career path of individuals.[68] One aspect of selection the literature leaves relatively untouched is the issue of the necessary formality and structure of selection versus individual flexibility; the literature provides no consensus on how best to allow people to move into and out of the pools while assuring the organization of needed talent. Little of the literature addresses how to balance manager identification of high-potential employees while maintaining opportunities for individual self-determination. When considering the developmental and advancement prospects in terms of the number of high-potential employees pursuing them, it is unlikely everyone will achieve his/her desired goals. For IC succession planners, managing employee expectations within organizational resource limitations can be yet another challenge.

---

65 Bennis, 184.

66 Bernthal and Wellins, 31+.

67 Ralph Bledsoe and others, *Managing Succession and Developing Leadership: Growing the Next Generation of Public Service Leaders* (Washington, DC: National Academy of Public Administration, 1997), link from URL: <http://www.napawash.org/publications.html>, accessed 11 July 2006.

68 Douglas T. Hall, "Dilemmas in Linking Succession Planning to Individual Executive Learning," in *Leadership Succession*, ed. Stewart D. Friedman (New Brunswick, NJ: Transaction Books, 1986), 70.

After crafting the process to select potential leaders, IC succession planners may turn attention to addressing the needs of those not identified as having potential for further advancement. For example, some of today's leaders and other solid, necessary performers for the organization should be kept motivated.[69] Incentives to keep these peak performers at their tasks may include assistance with identifying career paths for those without senior management responsibilities, continued access to development opportunities, or other motivations tailored to the needs and desires of the individual.[70]

Even those of us who never met a process we didn't like must acknowledge that no process is perfect. Internal improvement efforts must be considered an aspect of succession management.[71] Succession management will not succeed if it is merely a paper exercise that current leaders do not monitor. "Leaders are both architects and general contractors, and they should be judged not only by the elegance of their plans, but also by the quality of implementation and maintenance of the design."[72] In its report to Congress on the human capital practices of nine private-sector companies, GAO addressed measures of effectiveness. The report indicates that companies (for example, Sears, Roebuck and Company and Merck and Company, Inc.) use these measures to make decisions regarding policy and procedure changes. Merck managers consider the input of employees as to the effectiveness of its human capital initiatives.[73] Metrics upon which current leaders will assess the effectiveness of succession will have to be established before its implementation—yet another task for IC succession planners.

Tools of the Trade

The Corporate Leadership Council describes the data required for the General Electric (GE) "Session C" meetings as being minimal, including only the most pertinent personnel and organizational information needed to make decisions on succession and talent needs. Gathering information about employees within a business unit provides the CEO visibility into not only

---

[69] Jeffrey Sonnenfeld, "Heroes in Collision: Chief Executive Retirement and the Parade of Future Leaders," in *Leadership Succession*, ed. Steward D. Friedman (New Brunswick, NJ: Transaction Books, 1986), 116.

[70] Faye Cope, "Current Issues in Selecting High Potentials," *Human Resource Planning* 21, no. 3 (1998): 15+.

[71] Smith and others, *A Preliminary Evaluation of the NRO Succession Management Program*, 11.

[72] William C. Steere, Jr., "Leadership Challenges for Present and Future Executives," in *The Leader of the Future: New Visions, Strategies, and Practices for the Next Era*, eds. Hesselbein and others (San Francisco: Jossey-Bass, 1996), 269.

[73] U.S. General Accounting Office, *Human Capital: Nine Key Principles from Nine Private Sector Organizations*, Report to Congress, GAO/GGD-00-28, 31 January 2000, 17-18.

the available talent in that unit, but the employee development efforts used by the unit's leaders and supervisors. [74]

Employee information

Performance, potential, development, training

Organization information

Strategic direction, significant changes

Personnel issues (retention, diversity, movement, succession candidates) [75]

Data for GE's Session C, Leadership Talent Assessment.

Much as a multi-national corporation like General Electric requires semi-independent business units to gather personnel data to support the corporation, one might expect IC data gathering to be done by subordinate units of the multi-faceted Community, at the agency level, for example. The data provide visibility for the cross-organization succession management efforts—what positions are considered critical by each agency, how individuals are developed, and who are the potential future leaders.

Depending upon the size, companies may choose standard, Commercial Off-The-Shelf (COTS) HR platform packages with embedded tools to aid in succession implementation. Others may determine, as did the Pep Boys Company, that a web-based tool better solves the data gathering and organization problem. With approximately 20,000 employees geographically dispersed, Pep Boys selected an on-demand tool, allowing managers to input information regarding employees' performance, potential for advancement, and departure risk.[76] Oracle's PeopleSoft, used by some IC agencies, contains tools to manage the workforce; according to Oracle's website, the tools allow organizations to prepare for and get ahead of the expected baby boomer departures.[77] As some observers suggest, "Drawing direct parallels between

---

74 Corporate Leadership Council-Corporate Executive Board, *The Next Generation: Accelerating the Development of Rising Leaders*, 139-140.

75 Corporate Leadership Council-Corporate Executive Board, *The Next Generation: Accelerating the Development of Rising Leaders*, 139-140.

76 Drew Robb, "Succeeding with Succession: Tools for Succession Management Get More Sophisticated," *HR Magazine*, January 2006, 89-92.

77 Oracle "Applications for Talent Management Enterprise-wide," URL: <http://www.oracle.com/applications/manage-talent-enterprise-wide.html>, accessed 31 March 2007.

public- and private-sector research on succession must be done carefully."[78] Acquiring the best succession management tools for the IC may require more than simply procuring software packages. Succession planners may need to undertake an exhaustive search and evaluation process to ensure the most effective tools are obtained.

For evaluation and assessment, experts agree that no one method or tool is best. Rather, the consensus, particularly with respect to estimating potential, favors use of a variety of tools. In addition to multi-assessor ratings (or 360° evaluations), interviews by selection officials provide a more in-depth picture of the candidate's potential to satisfy the organization's leadership requirements for the future.[79] Rothwell recommends assessment centers be considered a valuable part of the evaluation process, as they can provide objective consideration of individuals against the stated organizational needs. [80]

IC succession planners may find each agency able to gather data on employees, but the terms and types of data, in addition to their format, may well vary by agency. ODNI has undertaken an effort to coordinate intelligence information sharing across the Community; perhaps succession planners could take advantage of this work to extend information-sharing capability to encompass pertinent personnel data. In any case, implementing succession requires information on the organization and the workforce; without it, little or no planning can be done.[81] IC succession planners need to explore the availability and efficacy of commercial and government-sponsored assessment centers.

Barriers

Although the case for managing succession was made earlier in this section, we may note that even broadly desirable change may meet with some resistance. Implementation of succession management is no exception. If the procedures associated with succession appear too difficult or time-consuming relative to the perceived benefit, managers and employees alike will resist fully embracing it; to combat resistance to implementation, the procedures must be "relatively simple and flexible."[82] Two other impediments include a

---

78 Ellen Schall, "Public Sector Succession: A Strategic Approach to Sustaining Innovation," *Public Administration Review* 57, no. 1 (1997): 4+.

79 McFee and others, *Leadership for Leaders: Senior Executives and Middle Managers*, 39-40.

80 Rothwell, 22.

81 Kettl and others, 15.

82 Thomas S. McFee and others, *Developing the Leadership Team: An Agency Guide*, of The 21st Century Manager Series, December 2003, 14.

preoccupation with today's issues and the related inability to see the potential return on investment for the future.[83] One mitigating strategy in the face of these barriers would reinforce the idea that succession ensures a positive legacy for current leaders, not only through selection of competent leaders for the future, but by reinforcing the organization's capabilities, which should be passed on to the next generations of professionals.[84] Also, if identifying the high-potential individual, which may be interpreted as favoritism, becomes an issue, communicating how succession management implementation will be conducted in a manner fair to current employees should also help minimize employee concerns. Explaining the intent and procedures of succession to new hires can minimize this resistance factor for the future.[85] Developers and those implementing IC succession management need to account for these general resistance factors, as well as any specific culturally based sources of resistance within the Community.

Basics in Hand

This review of leader, leadership, and succession literature provides basic information. One might be tempted to start constructing detailed plans for the Intelligence Community based on the information presented in this chapter. However, the results might prove un-executable. Industry practices may be used as guidelines, but legal and regulatory constraints must be the basis for federal personnel management plans. For the IC, the structure and fractured history of personnel efforts should serve as a caution. In developing and implementing succession management, the Community cannot avoid taking into account pertinent statutory requirements and the related implementation practices in place. These thoughts are developed in the next chapter.

---

83 "Succession Planning Facts and Fantasies," *Journal for Quality & Participation,* 22 September 2005, 5.

84 Schall, 4+.

85 Patrick Ibarra, "Succession Planning: An Idea Whose Time Has Come," *Public Management,* January-February 2005, 20.

CHAPTER 3
The Community

An organization that is not capable of perpetuating itself has failed. An organization therefore has to provide today the men who can run it tomorrow. It has to renew its human capital. It should steadily upgrade its human resources. [86]

The Mandate for a Plan

Given the importance of its mission, it should not surprise that the Intelligence Community would aggressively seek skilled leaders for senior positions. Even as the Intelligence Community was being formed, personnel management and requirements for leaders were included in founding documents. The National Security Act of 1947 characterized the national security intelligence apparatus as a community.[87] Beyond establishing the Community, this same Act provided the first personnel oversight authority for Community employees.[88] Also, it contained some specifications for those holding senior positions, such as rotational assignments. This offered the first reference to career requirements for senior intelligence leaders.

Twenty years later, Executive Order (EO) 11315, of 17 November 1966, recognized the expansion of responsibilities for federal senior leaders and the critical need to have the best personnel in these positions. The Order designated General Schedule grades 16, 17, and 18 as Executive Assignments and required procedures to assure qualified individuals were recruited, selected, and developed for these positions. EO 11315 required "improvements in the identification, assignment and utilization of key personnel." [89]

Just a decade later, the Civil Service Reform Act (CSRA) of 1978 established the federal Senior Executive Service (SES) with the intent of creating a cadre of highly proficient leaders directing the operations of the U.S. Govern-

86 Peter F. Drucker, *The Effective Executive* (New York: Harper & Row, 1966), 56.

87 National Security Act of 1947, PL 80-253 (Washington, DC, 26 July 1947).

88 The National Security Act of 1947, Section 104, states that management and personnel functions should be consolidated across the Community. The law gives the DCI authority for working with agency heads to develop and implement procedures and policy to enact this consolidation. It appears that the DCI from the beginning had the authority and responsibility to ensure consistency across the IC for personnel management.

89 U.S. President, Executive Order 11315, *"Amending the Civil Service Rules to Authorize an Executive Assignment System for Positions in Grades 16, 17, and 18 of the General Schedule"* (Federal Register, 1966).

ment. The CSRA required that the newly renamed Office of Personnel Management (OPM)[90] establish and maintain standards for appointment to and continuation in the Service. [91]

It may appear that the IC had been overlooked by the CSRA, given that it established an exception to the Senior Executive Service for organizations with missions to conduct foreign intelligence or counterintelligence activities. However, the CSRA indicated that these organizations must make efforts to establish equivalent requirements for senior leaders. Echoing that admonition, Title 5 of the United States Code Section 3132 asserts that these organizations "shall make a sustained effort to bring... personnel system[s] into conformity with the Senior Executive Service to the extent practicable."[92] The Code of Federal Regulations (CFR) 5 Section 317.501 affirmed that "recruitment and selection for initial SES career appointment [will] be achieved from the brightest and most diverse pool possible."[93]

Stating requirements for government executives, EO 11315 specified development and training for those in the Executive Assignment System. In 1967, EO 11348 mandated the continuing development of the entire workforce, requiring agencies to "[create] a work environment in which self-development is encouraged."[94] The CSRA required that the SES provide opportunities to its members for continued growth and development.

The Federal Workforce Flexibility Act of 2004 (referred to hereafter as the Flexibility Act) required that instruction be provided to supervisors in the handling of a variety of situations, preparing them for the difficulties of management; this training underlies the "comprehensive management succession program" described in amendments to the Flexibility Act.[95] The Flexibility Act indicated that training programs, in part considered succession management by this Act, assured availability of effective managers

---

[90] The agency now known as the United States Office of Personnel Management (OPM) is the federal agency that ultimately inherited the responsibilities directed to the Chairman of the Civil Service Commission by President Kennedy's 1961 memorandum pertaining to the oversight and coordination of Federal Executive Boards (FEBs) and Federal Executive Associations (FEAs). The Office of Personnel Management was created as an independent establishment by Reorganization Plan Number 2 (5 U.S.C. appended) effective January 1, 1979, pursuant to Executive Order 12107 of December 28, 1978. Many of the functions of the former United States Civil Service Commission were transferred to this new agency. The duties and authority are specified in the Civil Service Reform Act of 1978 (5 U.S.C. 1101).

[91] *Civil Service Reform Act of 1978*, PL 95-454, (13 October).

[92] "5 U.S.C. Section 3132," (GPO).

[93] "5 CFR Chapter 317, Employment in the Senior Executive Service," 182.

[94] U.S. President, Executive Order 11348, *"Providing for the Further Training of Government Employees,"* (Federal Register, 1967).

[95] *Federal Workforce Flexibility Act of 2004*, 108-411, 108th (30 October 2004), Section 201, Chapter 241.

within each agency.[96] The Intelligence Reform and Terrorism Prevention Act (IRTPA) of 2004 holds the Director of National Intelligence (DNI) accountable for assuring development of the workforce. According to the IRTPA, the DNI may implement any education and training mechanisms to ensure the workforce gains an understanding of the Community. Further, Title 5 Section 4103 states that agencies will provide training for the current workforce and ensure publication of the selection process. This same section encourages joint training efforts by agencies.

In addition to education and training guidelines set forth for the SES corps, laws, codes, and regulations also contain references to rotational assignments as a means for personnel development. For example, the National Security Act of 1947 empowered the DCI to coordinate with department and agency directors in the establishment and management of rotational assignments, with such assignments considered part of the promotion requirements for senior positions.[97] Instructions on the exchange of Senior Executives between organizations of similar type, including the requirement for details on their official status during and after such an exchange, can be found in 5 CFR Section 214.204.[98] Specifics of Senior Executive movement (reassignments, transfers, and details) are contained in 5 CFR Sections 317.901-903. These sections refer to both internal agency and cross-agency moves. [99]

For the IC, the IRTPA takes the measure further by authorizing the DNI to require that service in more than one IC organization be a component of development, even requiring such service for promotion eligibility.[100] Fungibility across or, at least a working knowledge of the Community, remains a fundamental requirement for our Senior Executives. The thoughtful and planned movement of personnel across organizations signals a healthy preparation process.

> **"**
> **Fungibility across or, at least a working knowledge of the Community, remains a fundamental requirement for our Senior Executives.**
> **"**

---

96 *Federal Workforce Flexibility Act of 2004.*

97 *National Security Act of 1947.*

98 "5 CFR Chapter 214, Senior Executive Service," 79.

99 "5 CFR Chapter 317, Employment in the Senior Executive Service," 188-190.

100 *Intelligence Reform and Terrorism Prevention Act of 2004*, 108-458, 108th Congress, 2d Session (17 December 2004).

The table below lists pertinent regulations and statutes. This sampling of laws and regulations demonstrates the breadth of support and guidance available to the IC as it pursues a formalized process for leader identification, preparation, and placement.[101] The idea of preparing and improving leaders and other critical personnel has a long history.

Type	Number
U.S. Codes	5 Chapters/Sections: 3132 10: 38, 81, 83 50: 401, 401a, 403-4
Federal Regulations	5 Chapters: 214, 317, 430 58 FR 48255
Public Laws (P.L.)	80-253, 86-36, 95-454, 108-411, 108-458
Executive Orders	11315, 11348, 12333, 12861

A Sampling of Legal Guidance. *Source: Compiled by Author.*

Despite the many legal and regulatory mandates to provide effective leaders for the Intelligence Community, there appear few specific guides to selection officials' choices. OPM has responded by developing Executive Core Qualifications (ECQs) to provide guidance for both individuals and their evaluators. The ECQs describe what skills, knowledge, and abilities are requisite for nomination to the Senior Executive Service.[102] IC succession management developers may leverage OPM's work and the guidelines and regulations described in this section to support efforts such as the DNI's Joint Intelligence Community Duty Assignment (JDA) policy. This policy establishes the requirement for individuals seeking advancement to work in an organization other than their parent or hiring organization at least once in their career and pursue training to enhance their Community comprehension.

---

101 For more thorough examination of applicable statutes and regulations affecting the SES and the history of federal civil service in general, the reader is referred to the working draft of the "OPM Senior Executive Service Desk Guide" (available upon request) and OPM's website "Biography of an Ideal" (*http://www.opm.gov/biographyofanideal/*), respectively.

102 Executive Core Qualifications (Washington, DC: Office of Personnel Management, 1 February 2007), URL: <*https://www.opm.gov/ses/ecq.asp*>.

Prudence Recommended

Although the federal SES may serve as the foundation for IC senior executive management, particularly for selection and development requirements, it can be improved. According to a study conducted by the National Academy of Public Administration (NAPA) at the request of OPM, oversight of federal government senior leaders—policy, procedures, and their management—is too highly dispersed. OPM serves as the lead for allocations, training, and qualifications for senior leaders; the Office of Management and Budget (OMB) oversees resource management of human capital; the Government Accountability Office (GAO) works human capital evaluation, performance, and accountability; and each department or agency manages the day-to-day functions of senior leaders. The NAPA study acknowledged that this dispersal has the positive effect of creating a checks-and-balance structure; however, it unfortunately ensures that no one organization or individual is accountable for leading and managing a process to ensure effective senior leadership.[103] The NAPA study highlights what has already been identified as an issue for IC senior leader management—the delineation of authority and accountability.

Improvements to SES management may be in the offing, however. With the signing of the Homeland Security Act of 2002, and the Chief Human Capital Officers Act of 2002, a baseline existed for better coordination of workforce development with strategic mission and human capital plans.[104] The President's Management Agenda (PMA) also called for improvement of the federal workforce through stronger human capital planning procedures.[105] OPM's work to satisfy these requirements continues, as demonstrated by the publication and on-line availability of the Human Capital Assessment and Accountability Framework (HCAAF), a series of documents and tools to assist managers and employees.

Succession Implementation at a Glance

Interviews conducted with IC experts provided an insider's perspective on implementing succession management—its prospective outcomes, the wheels for the machine, and its legal support.

---

103 Ingraham and others, *Strengthening Senior Leadership in the U.S. Government.*

104 *Homeland Security Act of 2002*, 107-296, (25 November 2002).

105 U.S. President, *President's Management Agenda*, (Washington, DC: Office of the White House, 2002), 11-13.

Getting Their Opinion

The informal interviews carried out for this study covered three broad areas affecting or affected by succession management: activities (past and current), beliefs (in workforce management), and compelling forces (for change or for the status quo). Interviews were conversational, providing the participants flexibility in responding to queries. This design provides for cataloging recurrent ideas from Community practitioners.

Preparing for the Interviews

To gain the greatest exposure to current views of succession management, the author interviewed individuals working at relatively high levels. Directors were excluded, as these individuals tend to have shorter tenures than career Senior Executives; the more appropriate subjects appeared to be those Senior Executives reporting to the Director and Deputy Director. Also, since the current paper focuses on the top three tiers of senior managers below the level of Director, interviewing the current cadre of senior managers held the potential to garner unique views on how their replacements might best be selected. To winnow the potential interview subjects, those holding positions most relevant to the development and implementation of succession management (the Community's experts) were identified as the most desirable subjects. Therefore, senior managers of operational or mission and support organizations do not appear on the potential interview list. Those on the final interview list were contacted using Intelink searches or third-party introductions (for example, introduction to a potential subject made by a member of the IC Executive Resources Forum).

Chief of Staff

Chief Human Capital Officer

Deputy Chief Human Capital Officer

Director of Executive Resource Management

Director of Leadership Development

Chief of Workforce Planning

Chief of Succession Planning

Positions Held by Subjects Interviewed. *Source: Author.*

Agencies represented include the Central Intelligence Agency (CIA), Defense Intelligence Agency (DIA), National Geospatial-Intelligence Agency (NGA), National Reconnaissance Office (NRO), and National Security

Agency (NSA). Additionally, representatives from the Office of the Director of National Intelligence and the Office of the Undersecretary of Defense for Intelligence participated in the research operation. The number of participants varied somewhat by agency. Subjects participated in one-on-one interviews with the author or in focus groups; two of the focus group sessions resulted in usable input from four subjects. One subject responded to questions via email.

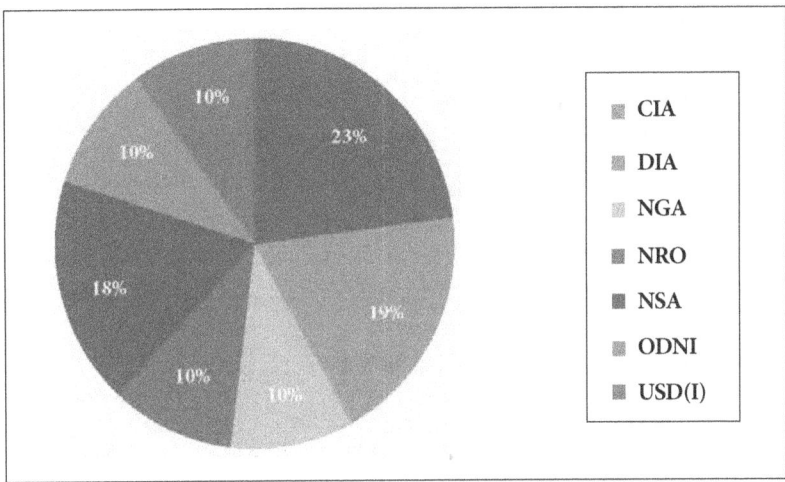

Interview Subjects by Agency (N = 21). *Source: Author.*

Questions provided insight into each agency in three broad categories: the history and status of succession, the culture, and the external factors affecting succession implementation. Information available via Internet and Intelink provided preparatory data for the interviews or provided answers to some interview questions. In instances where subjects provided responses without prompting, or the questions had been answered by other subjects from the same agency, the author modified the interview questions accordingly.

1. History and current process

a. How has your organization/agency approached top-echelon succession management (top three levels of senior executive leaders, but below the level of political appointees) over the last five years? How is it done now?

b. Who/what organization is the lead for succession management?

c. What tools are used to gather data for succession planning/modeling?

Interview Questions. *Source: Author.*

2. Agency culture

    a. What is the focus of your agency's documented workforce management strategy? How does it link to the agency's mission?

    b. What are the management trends or philosophies embraced by your agency?

    c. How could your agency improve its approach to succession management?

3. External factors

    a. What is your agency's participation in the various boards associated with workforce and/or executive succession management?

    b. With what private sector succession management plans and achievements are you familiar?

    c. What do you see as the external factors affecting succession management for your agency?

Interview Questions. *Source: Author.* (Continued)

The exceedingly candid subjects provided a large amount of information. The use of spreadsheets simplified the task of documenting and organizing the information for review and analysis. Once the results of all interviews were compiled into the spreadsheet, then organized by question and by agency, recurring phrases or statements stood out. These in turn became "themes." The spreadsheet below shows the method of grouping and counting themes. The following sections develop the recurrent themes for each category. Likert scores facilitated the capture of opinions regarding succession management maturity in the Community.

All told, the illustrative views expressed by subjects suggest intriguing avenues for subsequent testing and implementation of succession management.

Questions	Themes	Number of Responses
SM development in last five years?		
	Boards have been used	5
	Agency efforts to establish processes	10
SM Current?		
	Single individual selects SESes	4
	Board selection process	3
SM lead?		
	HR/HC	4
	Mission organizations (depends on level)	2
	Cross/multi-organizational (depends on level)	6
	Single individual cited as lead	3
SM tools (modeling)?		
	Specific tools for SM and/or general use	7
	Tools specific to SM only	2
Pool review frequency?		
	Of those citing pool existence, quarterly	2

History and Current Process: Interview Themes by Question. *Source: Compiled by Author.*

History

One category of questions aimed to gather historical data on succession management work at each agency. The responses provide insight into whether and with what success a subject's agency had attempted succession management. For both current and past efforts, subjects identified the lead—whether an individual or organization. In the instances where subjects acknowledged the existence of a candidate pool, they provided more information on the process of managing the pool; specifically, the frequency of reviewing those in the pool; considering candidates for the pool; and then identifying participants.

Although the first interview question requested that subjects describe succession management developments over the last five (5) years, some talked about changes over a longer time span (e.g., 10 years). The most consistently repeated response confirms the long-term existence of corporate-level efforts to establish processes for identification, selection, development, and/or promotion of individuals to leader positions. Subjects from five different agencies provided this response. The issue of succession or replacement identification has already become a part of the leader management and human capital efforts within some intelligence agencies. This situation indicates that the potential exists to draw on lessons learned in structuring a Community-wide succession management effort.

Gathering these lessons may serve two purposes. First, the opportunity to share experiences and make recommendations in a peer environment may draw support from those responsible for implementing Community succession. Second, by leveraging lessons learned, the new effort has a greater chance of success. As lessons are gathered, succession planners may be well advised to develop a common lexicon on the topic, despite subjects' familiarity with it. Since each agency may have approached the work differently, establishing a common lexicon would be a worthwhile undertaking before serious development work begins.

Of the 15 subjects asked about their respective agency's succession management, only five indicated past or current use of boards (see bar chart). This should not be interpreted to mean that the majority of subjects believed decisions regarding succession were made by a single individual or small, unofficial group within their respective agencies. Instead, the remaining subjects indicated that succession abides as part of overall personnel development efforts, as a delegated responsibility below the corporate level, or they were unclear how succession management is addressed.

Interestingly, the idiosyncratic selection of Senior Executives (GS15s for promotion to Senior Executive) by a single individual appears as a notable recurring theme in the area of current succession management. The perception is that the decision can be made legitimately, even if solely by the head of an agency or by a delegated individual. Interview subjects did not elaborate further on the decision-making process by a lone selection official. Even so, the limited occurrence of this response plus the undeniable authority that agency heads do have to make such determinations, may make it of little concern in the future development and implementation of succession management. Nevertheless, it serves as a warning for those engaged in succession management to communicate standard selection procedures to dispel any possible perception of favoritism.

Of those identifying the lead for current succession efforts, seven identified the responsibility as shared across one or more organizations (see chart on next page). Subjects placed a caveat on the shared responsibility for leading succession, depending upon the level in the organization. For example, succession of seniors might be determined or recommended

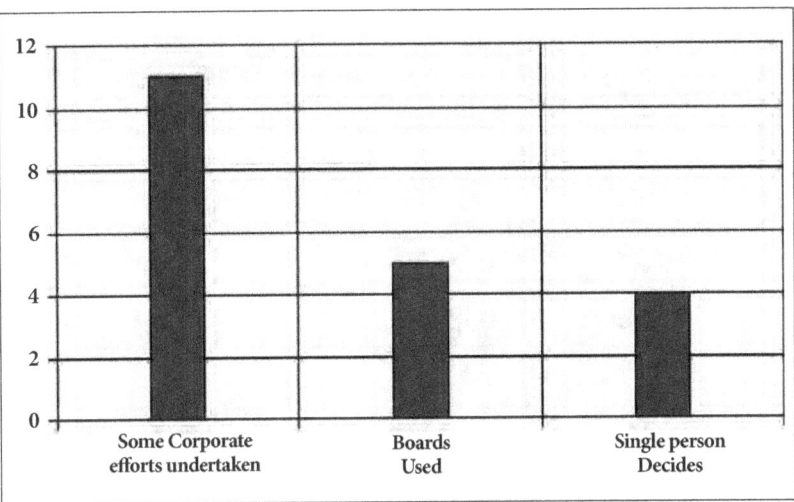

Recent Approaches to Succession Decisions. *Source: Compiled by Author.*

by a person on the agency head's staff, while succession for junior grades (13s and below) might be performed within an operational organization. Although subjects were told the nature of this paper (top three tiers of senior civilian leaders), some chose to broaden their responses to address all levels in the organization.

> "
> The idiosyncratic selection of Senior Executives (GS 15s for promotion to Senior Executive) by a single individual appeared as a notable recurring theme in the area of current succession management.
> "

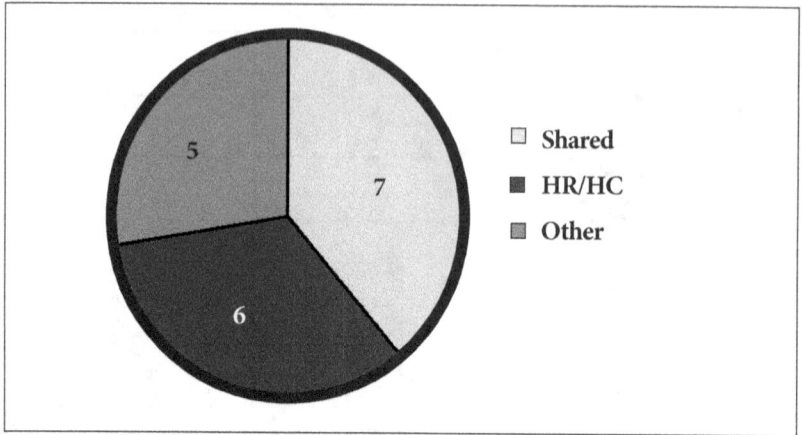

Current Agency Lead for Succession. *Source: Compiled by Author.*

The second most-often stated response was that the Human Resource/ Human Capital (HR/HC) organization takes the lead in current succession work. The impact of the operational organizations in determining the pipeline for or membership in a pool of future leaders cannot be underestimated in developing IC-wide succession management. However, with its broad view of skills and abilities needed by an agency and with experience in managing personnel processes, the HR/HC organization should play a significant role, as some of the literature indicates. If the responsibility for succession is to be shared, the roles for each organization should be unambiguous and accountability assigned. As the saying goes, "If everyone is responsible, no one is accountable."

In a question related to current procedures, subjects were asked about tools used for succession management. Only two subjects indicated tools exist exclusively for this purpose. The majority of responses describe tools used for broader workforce management (modeling, for example). This finding may prove significant as Community-wide succession management gains momentum, because it relies heavily upon data gathering and analysis (for positions and people). Some large, geographically dispersed, private-sector organizations use web-based tools to track employee performance and highlight potential leader candidates, as highlighted in the previous chapter.[106] Commercial software tools, such as PeopleSoft, offer embedded workforce management tools. The talent management tool industry is an expanding one—good news for organizations searching for help. [107]

---

106 Robb, 89-92.

107 "Plateau Systems Unveils Industry's First Enterprise-Class OnDemand Performance, Learning, and Succession Management Solution; Expanded Offering Will Provide Companies with Flexible and Affordable Best-in-Class Talent Management Solution," *Business Wire*, 13 June 2006.

Four subjects referred to the existence of a succession pool. When asked for further information about the procedures related to the pool, two indicated that a review of candidates (for example, additions to or removals from the pool) occurs on a quarterly basis. They went on to note that the reviewing officials in these cases varied depending upon the level or grade of those in the candidate pool; for example, a Senior Executive candidate pool would be reviewed by the senior leadership team, including the head or deputy of the agency.

It should be noted that not all subjects were asked directly about the existence of candidate or succession pools, as some responded without being asked. Also, once the existence (or lack of) pools was indicated for an agency, other subjects from that agency were not queried regarding the existence of a pool. The two who described continued use of a pool (including its periodic and formalized review) were from the same agency.

The rationale behind use or avoidance of a candidate pool in agencies' efforts is unknown. For future IC succession implementers, the willingness or resistance of agencies to adopt this approach to IC succession management should be considered. Regardless of the chosen process (pool or no pool), the supporting rationale should be documented and communicated throughout the workforce.

When asked to describe succession management policy efforts, 13 subjects from five different agencies responded that change or development was underway. Seven of the responses refer to the continuing maturity of the Joint Intelligence Community Duty Assignments policy enacted in 2006 by the Office of the Director of National Intelligence. A brief description of Intelligence Community Directive Number 601 appears below.

In accordance with the National Security Act of 1947, as amended by the Intelligence Reform and Terrorism Prevention Act (IRTPA) of 2004, and Executive Orders 12333 and 13355, the Director of National Intelligence establishes the policy and procedures to encourage and manage rotational assignment in more than one element of the IC. The intent is to create a greater understanding of the "variety of intelligence requirements, methods, users, and capabilities." These assignments will be required for promotion to certain key positions which "require and/or provide substantive professional, technical, or leadership experience in more than one IC element."[108]

Joint Intelligence Community Duty Assignments.

---

108 Intelligence Community Directive Number 601, Joint Intelligence Community Duty Assignments, Office of the Director of National Intelligence, Washington, DC, 16 May 2006.

If agencies are in the midst of a review or change process for personnel policies, those undertaking the establishment of IC-wide succession management may find less resistance than in a stable policy environment. However, the literature strongly suggests that one workforce attitude to be avoided is "here comes another one."[109] Juran suggests that employees and managers may become jaded with management fads; they may purposely or unwittingly doom efforts perceived to be just one more change in a never-ending series of management experiments. Also, with several subjects already citing ODNI policy and anticipating more such dispatches in the future, there is momentum for ODNI to lead development of IC-wide succession management policy.

Efforts have indeed been made to identify qualified replacements for leaders within the various agencies; however, participants' comments suggest failure or inadequacy of some efforts. Those attempting to implement IC-wide succession may be able to succeed if lessons are drawn from previous efforts to influence the development of new procedures. If individuals perceive a need for succession management within their own agencies but have little faith in the maturity of their existing process, the environment may prove ripe for adopting an IC-wide plan.

As noted in the literature review, succession efforts should not be rushed, but worked on a reasonable schedule of progress, identifying and following milestones. However, even a reasonable schedule must get underway. Now may be the best time to articulate and implement IC-wide succession management. A difficulty may lie in establishing Community procedures that encourage both those agencies well along in the process and those just beginning the endeavor.

Agency Culture

According to Schein, the ethnographer gathers information about the culture of interest from the perspective of an insider.[110] Using questions on workforce strategy, its link to mission, and current management trends, the present paper presents a preliminary, ethnographic view of IC agency cultures, the amalgam of which can provide insight into the IC's culture relevant to succession. The information provided by subjects may allude to opportunities to influence personnel policies and, therefore, opportunities to implement succession management. For example, an agency's workforce

---

[109] . M. Juran, *Juran on Leadership for Quality: An Executive Handbook* (New York: The Free Press, 1989), 77.

[110] Edgar H. Schein, *Organizational Culture and Leadership* (San Francisco, CA: Jossey-Bass Publishers, 1985), 21.

management strategy may reveal senior management's perspective on the value of employees and the approach taken to ensure that they make the greatest possible contribution to operations. Areas of commonality across the Community might suggest points to be leveraged early in succession development and implementation.

Of those asked about a workforce management strategy, eight agency representatives identified extant documents or on-going efforts to develop them (see Figure below). When asked to describe its focus, four representatives from three different agencies responded that the strategy underscores workforce development. This indicates the importance these agencies place on education, training, and/or developmental assignments for employees. For IC succession planners, this reinforces the literature's emphasis on establishing systematic development of leaders. It also provides an opportunity for consensus building across the Community, something IC succession developers may need to nurture.

It cannot be determined solely from the interviews if the workforce strategies emphasizing development reflect an agency's own character or if they stemmed from an externally-mandated template. It should be noted that some subjects used the term pool or *corps*, when referring to the entire *workforce* of the organization. Although there are various meanings for these terms, a clear distinction was not apparent in subjects' responses; the three terms seemed to be used interchangeably in this area.

Two other participants indicated the workforce management strategy with which they are familiar focuses on job or position requirements. Though small in number, these responses affirm that organizational needs, as expressed through the creation or continuation of a position, may take precedence over concerns for the individual. This echoes the catch phrase,

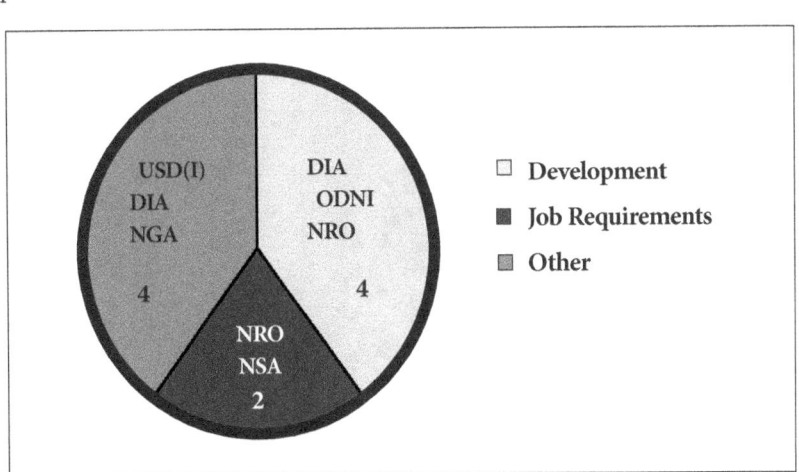

Workforce Strategy Focus. *Source: Compiled by Author.*

"Mission first." The prominence of mission in the workforce management strategy may indicate an area of divergence in the Community's approach to its employees, with some organizations touting personnel as "our greatest [and implicitly unique] asset," others treating them as a purely fungible commodity, and some mixing the two approaches.

The *intentional* linkage of workforce management strategy to mission or other agency-level strategic plans was not addressed by all subjects. However, interview responses and a review of information available online indicate that workforce management is frequently tied to mission strategy. As we have seen, some succession management literature highlights the importance of linking mission and succession to ensure that certain individuals are identified, prepared, and placed in jobs to achieve mission success.

Although agencies may tightly couple workforce management to mission requirements, succession management developers may be required to take a larger view and identify commonalities across the mission areas. These areas could be leveraged and incorporated into IC-wide succession management. For example, in defining *analyst* for the IC, each mission area may identify different development requirements for the advanced analyst; the succession planners' challenge is to identify common development requirements for the apprentice analyst. Based on discussion with USD(I) officials, on-going work in this area has resulted in a plethora of definitions; the succession planners may be able to assist in winnowing the list to a few, composite definitions for IC analyst. [111]

> In order to make a coherent, solid statement about culture, one has to gather and analyze data on the areas of consensus, patterns of perception/beliefs/emotions, and then decide whether there is no culture, a weak culture, or a thriving culture.[112] See next page for this paper's assessment.

Culture Examined.

44 |

111 Sources, senior-level intelligence professional at a national intelligence organization who wishes to remain anonymous, group interview by the author, 6 February 2007.
112 Schein, 111.

Alongside a workforce strategy, some agencies have a management trend or philosophy. Three subjects from two different agencies identified Lean Six Sigma as a basic guide for management. Others named continuous learning, merging of internal missions, or a debate about internal versus external hiring practices. Understanding an agency's management philosophy is akin to having the key to unlock effective communications. It will be important to tailor communication of succession's benefits and requirements using the terms of reference common to each agency. This knowledge will aid IC succession planners in identifying how to assist an agency in implementing new procedures or improving existing ones. Additionally, understanding how an agency approaches change may reveal how to address potential resistance factors. For those agencies without an espoused management philosophy, identifying potential change agents or champions may be the challenge.

- Areas of consensus or shared perceptions.
  - Extant or developing workforce management strategy: shared belief/ consensus
  - Focus of strategy: some cohesion
  - Management trends: almost no common ground
  - Succession Management ideal state: some shared perceptions, strong emotion
- The assessment:

In the area of workforce management, the IC culture remains weak, but has potential to thrive.

Workforce Management Culture in the IC. *Source: Author.*

Influencing the Process

To understand the level of engagement by the agencies in succession management, subjects were asked questions about their participation in related boards and familiarity with best practices in private-sector succession. Additionally, to identify current or potential impediments to succession implementation, subjects' opinions on that score were gathered. Finally, subjects were asked to identify any "external influences" on succession management improvement or implementation.

At the federal level and within the Intelligence Community, many boards exist to address human capital management topics, such as leader development and executive resource management. Most subjects (17 of

21) were asked about their familiarity with these boards and their agencies' lead participants in them. Of these, most (15) were aware of the boards and could identify their agency's participants. The majority cited their agency's representative as the Chief Human Capital Officer (CHCO) or his delegate. It should be noted that for some boards, department-level representatives attend on behalf of several agencies; some agencies rely on this departmental representation. Also, some of these groups are chaired by ODNI senior officials, some of whom were interview subjects. Some agencies already participate in fora on human capital issues. Succession management developers for the IC can take advantage of these groups to gain support, communicate expectations, and identify agency champions.

When asked about their familiarity with private-sector succession management, many (8) indicated having personal experience. Some subjects worked in the private sector before coming to government; others had researched private-sector methods of addressing HR issues. Subjects cited GE as a model for succession management six times. The three responses given most often after this were: IBM, government/private-sector contractor work (e.g., Development Dimensions International, Inc. (DDI)), and the military. The military is not the private sector, but the inclusion of this response should not be ignored in the exploration of succession management for the IC, as three subjects indicated experience with this model of succession management and considered it a valid one to emulate.

- For the individual
  - 360° assessment
  - Rotational, cross-organizational, and global assignments
  - Continuous development (Crotonville, NY training center)
  - Periodic, thorough review of candidates: determine development gaps and identify career path (promotability), and performance
- For the organization
  - Review (as part of periodic employee review) of changes in the organization
  - Identification of potential candidates for critical positions
  - Overview of HR initiatives
- Extensive executive involvement in the process
- Quasi-up-or-out approach (emphasis on delivered results)

The GE Approach. *Sources: Robert H. Bennett, III and others, "Today's Corporate Executive Leadership Programs: Building for the Future,"* Journal of Leadership Studies (1999): 3+ and Corporate Leadership Council, The Next Generation: Accelerating the Development of Rising Leaders, 1997.

All subjects provided opinions on factors influencing succession management implementation in the IC. The most frequent response (nine) was the influence of the Office of the Director of National Intelligence, specifically, the Joint Duty Assignment policy published in 2006. As seen earlier, this policy requires at least one cross-agency assignment for candidates aspiring to the senior executive rank. The second most-often cited response was that of the authority of ODNI to effect substantive changes. This response, given by four subjects, referred to unresolved legal issues regarding the roles and responsibilities divided between the ODNI and OSD, including matters such as human capital management. With the USD(I) now reporting to both the Secretary of Defense and the DNI, this issue may be less significant than at the time interviews were conducted.

The next most repeated influences each appeared three times in interviews. These include pay, culture, and talent competition. The repetition of pay and talent competition echoes succession literature, which suggests that increasingly, employers will be attempting to hire from a diminishing talent pool. Member agencies of the IC recognize the limitations of the government's ability to compete with the private sector in the area of salaries. It should be noted that not all responses were cited as impediments. For example, the JDA was considered a positive activity by at least four of the subjects. Several of the prominent influence factors identified by a varying number of participants are shown below.

Factors Influencing Succession Management. *Source: Compiled by Author.*

Participants considered ODNI a strong factor in succession manage-

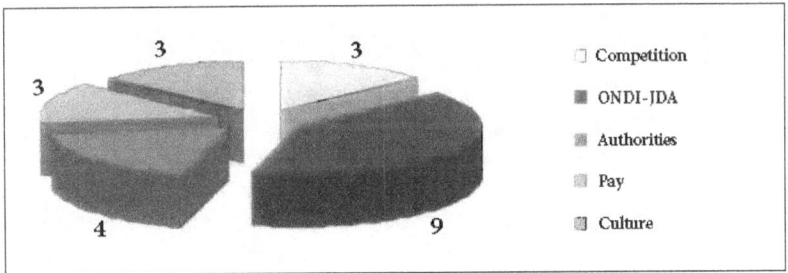

ment implementation, which indicates that ODNI enjoys a positive advantage in its coordination of succession management initiatives for the IC. Succession planners in the agencies should identify unresolved issues and bring them to the attention of those with the responsibility to settle them, rather than attempting to address issues that may be outside their own ability or authority to untangle.

Ideal Succession Management

Subjects were asked to describe improvements to current succession procedures or their notion of ideal succession management. They were not limited to considering their own agencies; however, subjects from ODNI and USD(I) were specifically asked to consider succession management for the entire IC. The following paragraphs provide the most often repeated phrases or concepts that emerged from the discussion.

About half of the subjects (10) linked some form of training and development efforts to improved or ideal succession management. One would expect this response from educators. However, this response came from representatives of a variety of organizations, including not only education and training, but human capital and executive resource management organizations.

Of the twenty-one subjects, nine described the ideal system as multi-tiered; for these subjects, the ideal system focuses not just on the senior executive ranks but on the middle and lower levels or grades throughout the organization. The use of rotational assignments was cited eight times. Roughly a third of subjects focused attention on the experience requirement for succession.

Four subjects suggested that the system contain a distinction between technical leaders and management leaders. For some this meant two distinct professional cadres.[113] Others described the two as complementary or parallel approaches; for example, as an individual develops technical prowess, he/she would be expected to pursue management or leadership competencies as well. [114]

Subjects considered professional development, whether for leadership or technical abilities, a basic component of succession. The definition of development here includes education, training, and experiential growth. To identify shared educational requirements across the Community may be difficult for succession planners without an accepted lexicon for the IC professions. The work done in this area has been taken into consideration, as the IC joint duty requirement now includes training for assignments. For IC succession planners, establishing criteria and mechanisms for gaining a breadth of experience will also be key. Taking into consideration responses to other questions, the implementation of the Joint Duty Assignment (JDA) stands out as a logical leverage point for ODNI coordination of Community succession management.

---

113 Name withheld, senior-level intelligence professional at a national intelligence organization, who wishes to remain anonymous, interview by the author, 14 November 2006.

114 Carolyn Conlan, Director IC Leadership Development Office (ODNI), interview by the author, 24 October 2006.

The Maturity Rating

Using a Likert scale consisting of five comparison statements, subjects ranked their own agency's succession management in three different ways. First, subjects provided a general assessment of their agency's succession maturity. Next, they compared it to private-sector succession management. Finally, they compared their agency's succession management to that of other government agencies. Since the intent of the question was to get a by-agency perspective on the maturity of succession management, the Likert scale was not an option for those subjects from ODNI and USD(I). Not only do these organizations' perspectives differ from those of the other subjects, whereby they view succession as an IC-wide issue, but each is a relatively new organization (less than two years old at the time this study was initiated) with little or no organic, internal succession process. One subject declined to complete the maturity ranking. Figure 12 shows the Likert scale given to subjects.

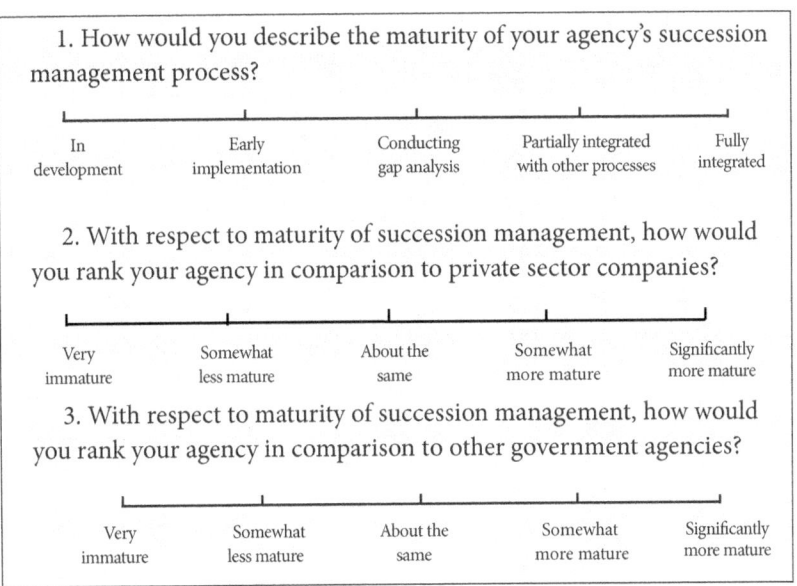

1. How would you describe the maturity of your agency's succession management process?

| In development | Early implementation | Conducting gap analysis | Partially integrated with other processes | Fully integrated |

2. With respect to maturity of succession management, how would you rank your agency in comparison to private sector companies?

| Very immature | Somewhat less mature | About the same | Somewhat more mature | Significantly more mature |

3. With respect to maturity of succession management, how would you rank your agency in comparison to other government agencies?

| Very immature | Somewhat less mature | About the same | Somewhat more mature | Significantly more mature |

Likert Scale. *Source: Author.*

In order to analyze the responses, each statement was given a numerical value from 1 to 5, with 1 as the lowest rating and 5 as the highest. Ratings are provided in the tablebelow.

Agency	How would you describe the maturity of your agency's succession management process?	With respect to maturity of succession management, how would you rank your agency in comparison to private sector companies?	With respect to maturity of succession management, how would you rank your agency in comparison to other government agencies?
DIA	1	1	2
	1	1	3
	1	2	1
	3	3	3
Average	**1.5**	**1.75**	**2.25**
NGA	2	1	3
	1	1	3
Average	**1.5**	**1**	**3**
NRO	4	4	5
	5	4	5
Average	**4.5**	**4**	**5**
NSA	0	0	0
	2	1	3
	1	2	3
	1.5	3	3
	1	2	3
Average	**1.4**	**2**	**3**
CIA	1	1	3
	1	1	3
Average	**1**	**1**	**3**
Likert Descriptors	1 = development 2 = Early implementation 3 = Conducting gap analysis 4 = Partially integrated with other processes 5 = Fully integrated	1 = Very immature 2 = Somewhat less mature 3 = About the same 4 = Somewhat more mature 5 = Significantly more mature	1 = Very immature 2 = Somewhat less mature 3 = About the same 4 = Somewhat more mature 5 = Significantly more mature

Succession Maturity. *Source: Author.*

To the question, "How would you describe the maturity of your agency's succession management process?" subjects most often selected "In development." The detailed, by-agency results reveal what may lie ahead for succession management developers. There is a perceived wide range in succession management maturity. Subjects from CIA indicated their agency to be in "Early development," with a rating of 1. Mean ratings for DIA and NSA were 1.5 and 1.4, respectively. DIA and NSA subjects believed their agencies to be beyond development but not yet in "Early implementation." The NGA mean demonstrates the perception that this agency is in early implementation. NRO subjects provided a mean rating of 4.5, by far the highest. The challenge for IC-wide succession planners will be to nurture those agencies in the fledgling phases of succession development without impeding the progress of those with more mature systems. The chart below shows the overall distribution of these responses.

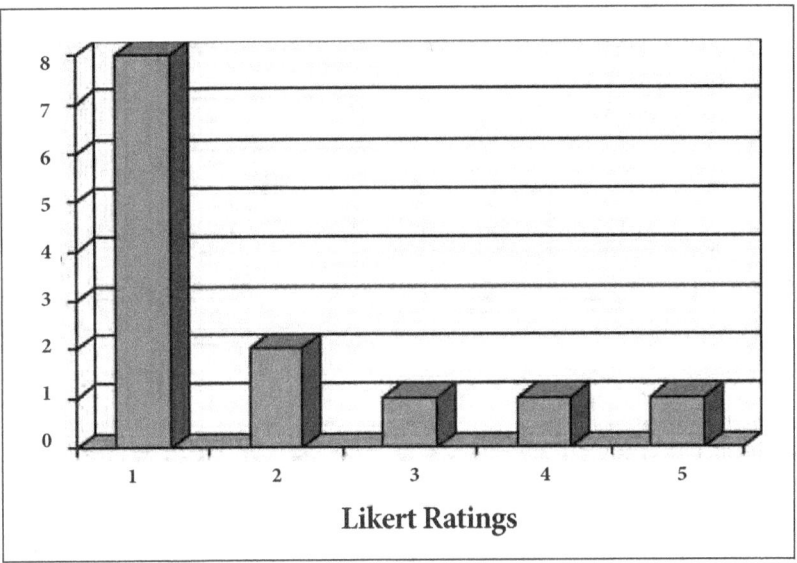

Perceptions of Succession Management Maturity. *Source: Compiled by Author.*

Subjects were given two measures against which to compare their agency's succession management—the private sector and other government agencies. Note that "other government agencies" was not further defined for subjects; some subjects may have interpreted the other government agencies as exclusively IC, while others may have considered the entire federal government. Also, the value of the private sector comparison ratings should be considered in light of previous responses indicating a subjects' familiarity with that sector.

Of the seven subjects who rated their own agency as "Very immature" in comparison to the private sector, four held significant knowledge of or gained experience in the private sector. The next most common assessment was "Somewhat less mature." Only one of these three individuals claims substantial knowledge of the private sector. "About the same" and "Somewhat more mature" were each cited twice. Each of these ratings was cited by one subject familiar with the private sector. The graphic below illustrates the participants' ratings.

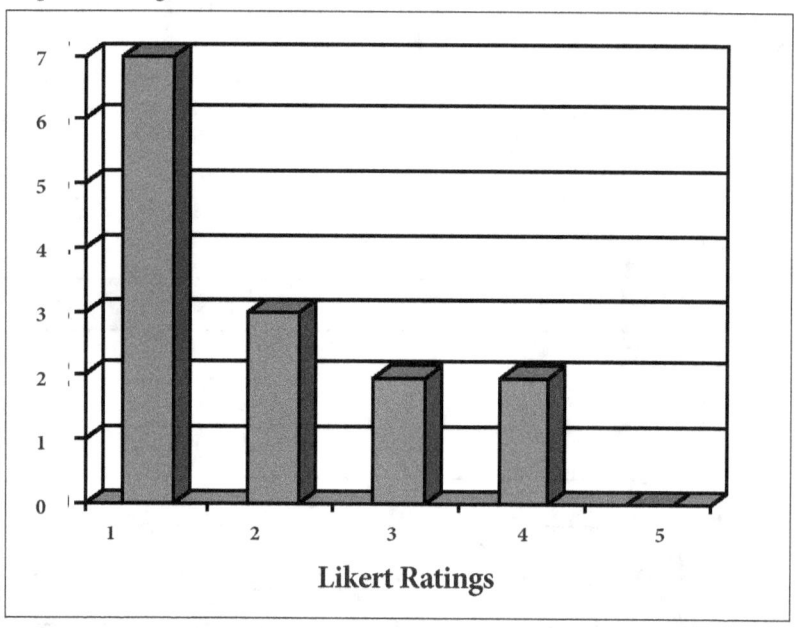

Comparison to Private Sector Maturity. *Source: Compiled by Author.*

The majority of interview subjects, including those familiar with the private sector, believe their own agency lags behind industry in addressing succession management. This finding suggests that the IC turn to the private sector for a solution or an operable succession management plan.

> **The majority of subjects believe their own agencies to be in the early stages of ... succession management.**

However, since some literature indicates that the private sector, too, has far to go in consistently and successfully implementing succession management, it may be more valuable to draw from the private sector for both successes and failures. A different interpretation may be that this assessment by interview subjects indicates an opportunity to partner with industry to advance the state of the art of succession management. In either case, this finding shows that these experts within the Community believe the IC must expend a great effort to achieve private industry's level of succession management maturity.

In comparing his/her own agency to other government organizations, participants most often indicated the two to be at equal levels of maturity. "About the same" appeared 10 times in 14 responses (see below). Further, the majority of subjects believed their own agencies to be in the early stages of development and implementation of succession management.

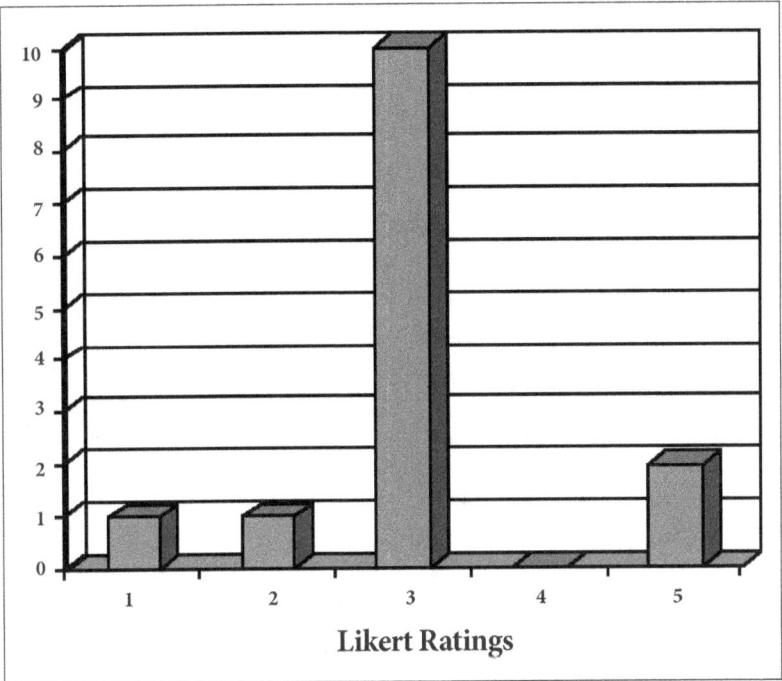

Comparison to Other Agencies' Maturity. *Source: Compiled by Author.*

Given that most subjects believed their own agencies are on par with other government organizations, one may infer that subjects perceive the rest of the federal government also to be in the same early stages of succession management work. One may also infer that most subjects, but not all, perceive the private sector to be more advanced than both their own agencies and the rest of government in succession efforts.

From an analysis of several studies and surveys, industry falls out as somewhat but not significantly better than the federal government in implementing some form of succession.[115] In the commercial intelligence sector, succession management focuses on the top tier of executives, rather than on

---

115 "Succession Management: Filling the Leadership Pipeline," *Chief Executive* (U.S.), April 2004, S1-4.

the levels below Vice President, which are the levels inhabited by the commercial intelligence professionals. [116]

To establish a baseline for IC succession management, developers have access to recent private-sector and federal government succession management benchmarking.[117] From the present study, assuming that knowledgeable subjects assessment of their own agencies' succession achievements is correct, developers have considerable opportunity to influence and leverage the succession process all across the Community.

What It Means

Succession management developers will find IC agencies willing to consider procedures that ensure development of the workforce, both to satisfy mission requirements and future leader needs. Some agencies have already started, and those not actively engaged in developing procedures are at least considering what could be done in the success arena. With so much human capital activity already underway in IC agencies and across the federal landscape, now is the ideal time to influence succession management. Still, even after agency and Community buy-in for the succession effort, IC developers face the same challenges as the private sector—creating an environment that systematically and effectively attracts, prepares, and retains individuals willing to assume leader positions.

Chapter Four outlines actions available to prepare the Community for succession management. To set the stage for these actions, those agency positions suitable for succession management, described earlier as the top three tiers of civilian personnel below the level of political appointee, are identified in the following table.

[116] A source, Member of the Society of Competitive Intelligence Professionals (SCIP), who wishes to remain anonymous, telephone interview by the author, 15 February 2007.

[117] The Corporate Leadership Council and Development Dimensions International have conducted private sector benchmarking efforts and are both familiar organizations to some in the IC. For federal benchmarking, RAND and the National Academy of Public Administration provide information relevant to succession management. In addition, GAO has investigated personnel policies of some U.S. and foreign government organizations. These represent just a few of the many sources available.

Agency Leaders	Mission or Supporting Leaders	Senior Leaders

Deputy Director
Chief of Staff
Chief Human Capital Officer
Chief Information Officer
Directors & Deputy
  Directors:
Directorate for Analysis
Directorate for Research
Directorate of Information
Technology
	President, Deputy and
	  Chief Academic Officer
	  of Community-oriented
	  education or training
	  office
	Directors & Deputy
	  Directors:
	Directorate for Security
	  & Installation
	  Operations
	Directorate of Foreign
	  Affairs
	Directorate for Advanced
	  Systems and Technology
		General Counsel
		Inspector General
		Chief Financial Executive
		Acquisition Executive
		Directors & Deputy
		  Directors:
		Office of Equal Employment
		  Opportunity & Diversity
		  Management
		Office of Congressional
		  & Public Affairs

Notes

1. Titles have been used, with permission, from DIA, NGA, and NSA. Although CIA and NRO did not provide example positions, those shown here represent the types of positions most likely to be considered among the top three tiers of senior leaders at these agencies.

2. Although considered leader positions, those clearly military have been excluded, such as Military Executive and Senior Enlisted Advisor.

3. Unless a requirement to have military assigned to a particular position could be confirmed, leader positions were included regardless of the incumbent's status (military or civilian).

Illustrative Positions Affected by Succession Management. *Source: Compiled by Author.*

CHAPTER 4
What Tomorrow Holds

"If we fail to get the workforce issue right, our overall attempt to position the community for the future will fall short." [118]

Each agency has tried or is trying to implement programs to develop the best possible leaders, but a central focus of external criticism remains a lack of cohesiveness in the Community. The stage is set for *someone* to do *something* to ensure that the collective intelligence organizations address shortfalls together. The existing laws, codes, regulations, and Executive Orders reviewed in this paper give ODNI the responsibility to unify and set personnel standards for the IC—to create and implement a plan through which to identify, prepare, and select future Community leaders.

This returns us to our original question: *How can the DNI advance the IC toward implementing succession management?* The literature and interviews offer some insights into actions the DNI and the Community may reasonably take to prepare for succession management: establish consistency for the Community, allow tailoring to mission-specific requirements, and delineate individuals' roles and responsibilities.

The box on the next page outlines a strategy to achieve consistency across the Community.

---

118 Vice Admiral L.E. Jacoby, USN, and Louis Andre, *Revitalizing and Reshaping the Workforce: A White Paper from the Joint Staff* J2 (Washington, DC: Department of Defense, 2000), 13.

- Consistency across the Community
  - Create the vision
  - Define leadership requirements
  - Manage leadership positions
  - Identify leadership development strategies
  - Specify evaluation and selection procedures
  - Provide a common lexicon
  - Effect the change
  - Mediate issues
- Tailoring or Mission Requirements
  - Facilitate technical and leadership training
  - Advise agencies on succession management
  - Assist communication of the message
- Individuals' Roles and Responsibilities
  - Offer tools for self-discovery
  - Publish information
  - Encourage and incorporate feedback
  - Support retention efforts

Community Strategy for Succession Management. *Source: Author.*

Establishing Consistency

Succession management literature advocates a strong linkage between an organization's mission, its vision, and its succession plan. Such a linkage ensures that future senior leaders selected as a result of succession management have the skills and experiences needed to achieve the mission. In addition to their selection, the future leaders' placement in positions drawing on their training and experience carries equal importance.

Early DNI actions would produce a long-term Community vision for Intelligence. Uniting behind this vision for tomorrow's intelligence, the Community may then establish leader requirements or competencies critical to achieving that vision. The DNI may even wish to identify or certify those critical positions in which future senior leaders may be placed.

> Although not expressly a succession tool as defined in the present paper, DIA's GEMSTONE program offers employees tools and opportunities to develop their competency as leaders. Rather than being tied to rank or grade, the four-tier program links professional development opportunities to roles or positions, such as team leader or supervisor. GEMSTONE allows for developmental opportunities beyond traditional training courses, to include skill application. Based on directorate-defined requirements (or competencies), directorate ranking of program candidates, and the inclusion of experience and other development touchstones, GEMSTONE may prove to be an illustrative component of any Community program to implement succession management.

Today's DIA. *Source: Author.*

Though a single, best definition of "leader" may not exist, future leaders may be identified through traits, behaviors, and anticipated environmental factors. IC succession planners may draw from OPM's SES Executive Core Qualifications (ECQs) and the IC Leadership Competencies developed by ODNI to advance this initiative. Using this extant work would allow succession planners to focus on documenting linkage of ECQs and Leadership Competencies to the IC-endorsed vision of Intelligence. This activity may be viewed as establishing the outcome expected from IC succession management.

The DNI can gain Community consensus on senior leader positions within each IC organization by identifying criteria vital to implementation of the Intelligence vision. In addition to identifying the critical positions (the priorities for the succession effort), ODNI may gain agreement on each organization's developmental positions (used to expand the experience of the current and future IC leader cadre). This task can be accomplished concurrently with defining leader requirements. For succession implementers, critical positions about to be vacated will likely attract the greatest and most immediate attention.

As the literature suggests, once these positions have been identified, planners should examine the work encompassed by each position, whether it should retain its current definition and status, or whether the position should be restructured so that others assume its responsibilities and duties. For developmental positions, this work has already begun. The DNI's Senior

> **"**
> **Although the academic and applied literature tends to emphasize the importance of experience . . . traditional preparation, such as classroom learning, remains necessary to fully develop leader skills. .**
> **"**

Officer Management Office (SOMO) has asked IC organizations to begin identifying developmental assignments to aid in implementing the JDA directive. Positions to be identified for the Leader Exchange and Assignment Program (LEAP) may be the first result of this work. IC succession planners can initiative cyclical review of both developmental and expert (mission-critical, non-developmental) positions.

Although the academic and applied literature tends to emphasize the importance of experience as part of the leader development process, it is clear that traditional preparation, such as classroom learning, remains necessary to fully develop leader skills. The vast array of opportunities in the Community for classroom learning suggests that Intelligence organizations agree. However, the wide spectrum of available training may require IC succession planners to single out those courses that are most critical for senior leaders and their candidate replacements. Demonstrating how all these developmental requirements are used in the senior leader selection process will also help instill trust in the workforce and aid selection officials in executing their task. Finally, leader development balances growth assignments, classroom training, and jobs in which future leaders apply what they have learned.

> With a new Director for CIA came new guidance on leadership management. General Michael V. Hayden, USAF, determined that a more corporate approach to the critical subject of leadership was needed. Since his arrival, corporate governance has been implemented, there have been changes in Senior Intelligence Service evaluations (new expectations have been defined and performance objectives have been aligned with Strategic Intent) and the Leadership Development Initiative was established for a systematic, Agency-wide effort to develop current and future leaders. The picture is clear—leadership is important to the Director of CIA. [119]

CIA's Direction. *Source: Author interview.*

---

[119] Name withheld, senior-level intelligence professional at a national intelligence organization, who wishes to remain anonymous, interview by the author, 22 February 2007.

The literature points out that managing the development of future leaders should be closely linked to the evaluation and identification of potential in individuals. The particular development recommendations for senior leader candidates should be tied to their knowledge or experience gaps as they relate to the needs of the Community. In short, leader growth should be orchestrated, not left to chance. IC succession planners may consult the IC Executive Resource Management group and its counterparts to learn how to address such difficult questions as the balance between manager identification and self-nomination of leaders.

Those who have studied succession management strongly suggest using a variety of methods to identify a potential leaders' abilities. Past performance may be used, but should be only one aspect of determining an individual's suitability for selection to a position of greater responsibility. As noted earlier, 360° reviews offer useful insight into an individual's behavior and performance. Interviews may be used to further tailor the selection process to the position at hand, and also may be used for identifying a general potential for professional growth. Formal assessment centers provide an objective evaluation of abilities and behaviors. ODNI may require IC succession planners to include these evaluation methods in the leader identification and selection process. IC succession planners should be tasked to provide the step-by-step processes to be used for development and selection to senior-most leader positions. These processes may mirror GE's Session C meetings, NRO's quarterly reviews, or some other method. Regardless of the actual steps, it should, as the statutes require, be published to educate the entire workforce.

Though past performance, as the literature suggests, may not be the best indicator of future achievement, the ability to assess performance and provide feedback are components not only of the selection process, but also of retention. With regard to past performance evaluation, it should be noted that the succession literature reviewed here makes no direct comment on how to accommodate or consolidate variations in procedures within an organization, such as exist among the IC agencies. With ramifications stretching beyond succession management, the standardization of performance evaluation across the Community may be an issue best addressed by an individual or group other than IC succession planners. Efforts already underway by the ODNI to establish performance requirements for senior intelligence executives may be emulated by agency succession planners.

As earlier highlighted, the USD(I) has started to create a dictionary of shared terms for the intelligence occupation. This effort may begin to establish, at last, the practice of intelligence as a formal profession, par-

> **"** Succession planners ... ensure technical qualifications are used to facilitate developmental assignments, not limit them. **"**

ticularly if supported by DNI. As the succession literature indicates, having objective criteria for evaluation of both performance and potential forms the basis of the process. Having common terminology across the Intelligence Community would aid in establishing these criteria by providing for consistency in discussions of technical ability as well as leader ability. Synchronizing the common lexicon and IC leadership competencies may mean that the leaders of the future are identified as technical leaders, management leaders, or "double majors"—those with the capability to lead in both contexts.

In today's specialized environment, it may repay succession planners to ensure technical qualifications are used to facilitate developmental assignments, not limit them. For example, although it may be difficult to identify growth assignments for those in specialized fields, their development should not be limited by their technical abilities. Rather than creating waivers, establishing a variety of methods to gain a broad perspective of the Community can facilitate personal and professional growth for all IC employees.

Interviews show that numerous agencies have attempted to develop and place well-prepared individuals in leader positions. Nonetheless, few of these efforts have incorporated succession management best practices. Still, DNI succession planners can benefit from lessons learned as well as from a review of relevant OPM and IC workforce surveys. Having one or even a few good reasons and embedded champions for change may not be enough to overcome cultural resistance factors. IC succession planners may need to dig deeply into each agency's management culture to determine how best to assist agencies in moving forward with IC-wide succession.

To introduce and carry out good succession management practices, interview subjects pointed to the utility of statutory authorities and comparative perceptions of private sector and military succession procedures. If some issues do not lie within the charter of the DNI succession management planners, the DNI-USD(I) relationship may be an effective medium for leveraging issue resolution and succession implementation.

As agencies refine their internal procedures and participate in cross-Community activities, DNI may be required to play a moderating role—resolving issues and providing clarifying guidance. The individual or group that the DNI designates to develop succession management for the IC may identify issues for elevation to a higher authority, with recommendations on how to resolve them. For example, an agency's technical skill requirements may limit the number, quality, or seniority of positions deemed suitable for leader development, and IC succession planners might highlight this anomaly for Community senior leaders to address. This may be the most expedient way to focus on succession without becoming bogged down in political debates.

<blockquote>
IC succession planners may need to dig deeply into each agency's management culture to determine how best to assist agencies in moving forward with IC-wide succession.
</blockquote>

Defensible succession planning for the Community will feature:

> ➤ Defined leader competencies, linked to mission/strategy and leadership positions
>
> ➤ An established, iterative methodology for identification and review of critical leadership positions
>
> ➤ A managed process for development of future leaders—using both experience and training
>
> ➤ Institutionalized procedures for assessing current performance and future potential
>
> ➤ Formalization of intelligence as a profession, requiring technical and leadership development
>
> ➤ An established mechanism for issue resolution
>
> ➤ A published implementation plan, including a communication strategy

Consistency Criteria. *Source: Author.*

In addition to highlighting the sources of general resistance to change, the succession literature points out a few, specific arguments against formal succession planning. DNI may best address such arguments through a thoughtful communication strategy—explaining the rationale for and details of implementing Community-wide succession planning. Ultimately, a transparent, effective process and its forthright implementation will provide the best response to all naysayers. It should be noted that interview subjects, almost without exception, were at least aware of numerous groups working various issues related to leader succession. DNI planners can thus expect that these groups can be useful in crafting and delivering the message about succession management. For example, DNI may call on IC Executive Resource managers, a group which meets quarterly to discuss Senior Executive issues, to advance work already underway on IC senior management, such as standardization of evaluation criteria and JDA requirements for senior executives.

Allowing For Agency Tailoring

Although planning for succession management should build in repeatability and consistency, there are some elements of the process that the Community may agree are appropriate for tailoring by agencies and organizations. Agency personnel do need unique technical skills to prosecute their missions effectively, and they can and do obtain home agency training in technical specialties. To enhance this training, DNI may offer support for special projects. Also, where educational communities of interest exist, DNI may aid in leveraging extant training opportunities for all agencies. For example, training in critical thinking would be beneficial for analysts, regardless of their mission area or parent agency. It should be noted that the requirement already exists for agencies to set aside approximately 25% of available seats or slots in courses for individuals from other agencies. DNI can help assure effective communication regarding these opportunities, so that classes are filled with those most in need of training.

> **Just as the IC uses rotational duty for development, agencies may . . . offer rotational assignments across internal organizations, particularly for junior personnel**

Just as the IC uses rotational duty for development, agencies may find it appropriate and beneficial to offer rotational assignments across internal organizations, particularly for junior personnel. For example, to gain a better understanding of how consumers use intelligence products, an apprentice-level author of such reports may be assigned to work with the consumer's on-site representative. IC succession planners may offer advice on how to manage such assignments. Also, when agencies choose to so develop junior personnel, the DNI may find it necessary or constructive to link it to the IC senior leader succession process and its Community rotational assignment requirement.

Interview results suggest that succession should be engaged as a process that addresses all organizational levels and grades, not just senior executives.

Almost half of the subjects explicitly confirmed this in their description of ideal succession management. Agencies should be free to implement internal procedures, pushing succession management to the most junior grades, thus providing grassroots input for the IC-wide process. In turn, ODNI may assist agencies in defining processes that ensure consistency in the areas of leader potential, experience evaluation, and advancement selection. However, because of technical specialization within each agency, some aspects of the process, such as assessment criteria for individual performance and potential in a technical field, should be determined by respective agencies.

ODNI may find it necessary to ensure that IC-wide leadership requirements are explicitly included as part of each agency's succession management implementation. Just as the literature indicates that subordinate business units are responsible to the corporation for developing and selecting future leaders, so should Intelligence organizations be responsible to the entire Community enterprise for internally preparing and placing leaders.

NRO's Succession Management Program (SMP) already has components of best practices in place. After 9/11, NRO's leadership expanded work already underway to better manage the distribution of skills (people) needed to accomplish the agency's mission. With help from a variety of sources—tool developers, private sector benchmarking, and senior leaders—the program grew. The SMP provides tools to employees to view and apply for vacancies as well as to document their skill sets. For managers, the quarterly review of critical positions and expected vacancies allows identification (or validation) of personnel needs; in addition, the agency-wide database of skill sets helps managers assess candidates for positions and verify the abilities of those applying for vacancies. Though SMP may be characterized by some as only a distribution center for talent, its combination of position and personnel databasing, management use of on-line tools, and transparent review and nomination processes, establish it as a powerful tool for managing personnel. The next phase of SMP expansion and improvement will likely be watched with great interest around the IC (and the private sector). [120]

On a Different Plane at NRO. *Source: Author interview.*

---

[120] Source: Name withheld, interview by author, 3 November 2006

The most effective way to communicate an IC-wide succession management plan to the workforce will be to align the message closely to each agency's distinctive workforce and culture. For example, one agency may promote the idea to employees that IC-wide succession is a way for employees to advance more quickly than in the past. Another may suggest that it is a way for the agency to gain the attention of and increase credibility within the Community and among stakeholders. The delivery methods, too, may vary by agency: some may welcome blogs while others prefer small, frequent town meetings. Although it emphasizes how to get the message to employees, the succession literature does not find any one method that might work best.

Finally, succession tools and data management may be tailored to an agency's particular information needs. Having simple tools available to the entire workforce—from selection officials to new hires—minimizes the "it's too hard" complaint that the literature cites as a common resistance factor. Although credible (even if not 100% accurate) data and easy workforce access to it are critical for succession management, IC succession planners may find that standardization of all succession tools remains beyond their ability or authority.

An agency may:

➤ Implement technical training, specific to mission requirements, sharing where there are IC communities of interest

➤ Implement an internal leader development program, including intra-agency rotational assignments

➤ Incorporate IC requirements into internal succession management procedures

➤ Shape the IC succession management communication strategy to reflect the needs of the workforce

➤ Establish tool acquisition and data management projects to produce internally and IC-required output

---

Agency Tailoring Criteria. *Source: Author.*

Defining The Individual's Role and Responsibility

It is easy to overlook the fact that the IC, like the rest of the federal government, is a human enterprise, and not an impersonal, purely bureaucratic mechanism. The IC comprises thousands of individuals, each with his/her own talents, concerns, and questions. One question to be expected from these individuals, particularly with respect to a change in personnel procedures, is "What does this mean to me?" As suggested below, DNI can begin to answer this question even as that process is being developed.

As the literature indicates, self-knowledge forms the basis for individual response to and participation in succession. In terms of professional development, a meaningful approach to determining one's own strengths and weaknesses is honest self-evaluation. To assist IC employees, DNI may review the self-evaluation tools currently in use to ensure that a variety is made available and easily accessible. For example, for both performance and potential evaluation, the 360° assessment is highlighted in much of the literature. In addition to using leverage to make this management tool widely available, ODNI can explain how the results might be used by individuals to determine where they need further development. The same explanation should be provided for each tool suggested by the DNI.

Leadership Effectiveness Inventory (LEI)[121]

360° evaluations

Individual Development Plans

Myers-Briggs Type Indicator (MBTI)

Self-assessment tools. *Source: Compiled by author.*

Self-examination can consider not only knowledge and abilities, but also behaviors or situational responses. The assessment of actions and reactions in a variety of situations may identify gaps in one's behavioral repertoire. The literature indicates that those aspiring to be leaders should have a diversity of approaches upon which to draw in order to operate effectively in the ambiguous and complex environment of senior managers.

In terms of career goals, the literature also indicates that generational differences impact the definition of success. However, just as the IC is a diverse consociation, so too is each generation a collection of unique individuals. For career paths, one size does not fit all. In addition to adopting self-examination for professional development purposes, each IC employee can be encouraged to discover and express his/her unique professional aspirations.[122] DNI may identify methods to help employees verify or discern their career goals. In turn, by articulating their professional development

---

121 Bledsoe and others, *Managing Succession and Developing Leadership: Growing the Next Generation of Public Service Leaders,* 149.

122 Bennis, 3.

needs and personal definition of success—whether higher pay, more power, greater influence—employees determine their level of participation in and dedication to IC succession management.

Personal insight will only be useful, however, if the employee has access to and understands the procedures and requirements of IC succession management.

Individuals self-nominate for a Joint Intelligence Community Duty Assignment (JDA) through the Agency's Human Resource Information System. The application includes both the supervisor's and individual's evaluation of critical leadership competencies. After a selection committee review, individuals ready for assignment are placed in a JDA pool, from which they are chosen as billets and assignments become available. Given the requirement for a joint assignment in order to be promoted to senior executive ranks, the JDA pool becomes the de facto succession pool for senior executives. In addition to identifying these high-potential individuals, NGA will conduct a review of positions or "occupations" to determine those most critical to the agency's success. Initially, succession management will focus on these positions. The opportunity to watch this proposal work through the approval process may provide IC succession planners some generally applicable lessons in communication strategies and business case development.

NGA's Human Development (HD) Directorate has a draft proposal for implementing succession management. *Source: Author.*

Some may prefer that information be "pushed" to them—suggesting that emails or paper materials be sent to employees. Others may prefer to pull data by making calls to their social network or searching on-line. Those charged with implementing a succession plan can bridge the gap between succession mechanics and employees' needs.

Additionally, some literature suggests that those developing and implementing succession management consider employee input to improve the process and increase the likelihood of its realization. In the definition stages, as DNI and IC developers lay the groundwork for procedures of succession management, they may use focus groups or individuals of both junior and senior ranks to capture concerns and suggestions about how IC succession should be structured. During the implementation phase, employee feedback will highlight areas for improvement, keeping the process current with changing employee expectations and needs.

The succession literature indicates that getting individuals engaged in the process adds to the probability of success. The newly established Senior Executive Management Organization at NSA takes this suggestion seriously. This organization recently sent a survey to current senior executives, asking: What do you want? What do you need? Who follows in your footsteps? When? Results from the survey are already being used to guide the placement and development of senior executives. The process moves NSA away from a self-identified wish list to validated, enterprise-wide needs and plans. Ultimately, the goal is to consider everyone's needs, those of the corporation and of the employee.

What a Senior Wants at NSA. *Source: Author.*

One word above all applies to individual expectations—realism. The literature confirms that not everyone enjoys the native abilities or development capacity to rise to senior-most ranks. In the IC, though the detailed figures are classified, there are surely a larger number of bright, highly skilled individuals than there are leadership positions for them to assume. For individuals, this recommends the development of realistic self-identified goals and perhaps a "Plan B" if career objectives will not be met by the IC. The ODNI and individual IC organizations still need to identify incentives to retain these strong performers who can make unique contributions to the intelligence mission.

We may expect individuals to:
- Define career and life goals
- Identify strengths and weaknesses (areas for further development)
- Stay current on internal and IC succession management changes
- Provide constructive feedback to managers and succession management implementers
- Be practical (realistic)

Criteria for Defining the Individual's Role. *Source: Author.*

The Nutshell

To advance the Community toward implementing succession management, the DNI and the entire workforce—career senior executive to new junior grade—can work collaboratively and singularly to ensure that well-considered succession becomes part of our cultural heritage. The next chapter reinforces the importance of succession management to the IC.

"If you do not know where you are going, every road will get you nowhere."

— Henry Kissinger

CHAPTER 5
Bringing Closure

Recap

Much has changed in the Intelligence Community over the last 20 years. For example, during the first Gulf War, the use of intelligence in shaping battlespace became the subject of evening news reports, a far cry from its previously obscure status. The hiring and fiscal boom of the 1980s gave way to the perceived shift in post-Cold War mission and associated budget reductions of the 1990s, requiring cuts across the IC. The public's increasingly voracious appetite for technology, stimulated by cell phones and the global pervasiveness of the Internet, may be characterized as a challenge, if not a threat, to the IC's mission. Following 9-11, an apparent lack of cooperation or integration within the IC was the topic of both media and expert attention and Community reflection. Not surprisingly, with these events as backdrop, the Intelligence Community leadership terrain has become more difficult to traverse.

Observing the operation of IC leaders in this increasingly fluid and intricate environment—of growing demands for quality and quantity of output; intensifying scrutiny by stakeholders on budget, mission, and management; and changing relationships within the Community—served as impetus for the current paper. The genesis of this paper was the perception that the IC had no process by which to identify and prepare future leaders to successfully navigate such a dynamic work setting. This problem statement was captured in the question, *"How can the DNI advance the IC toward implementing succession management?"*

Leaders who:

- Continually hone leadership skills
- Operate with a presumption of community in the Community
- Create benefit from interconnectedness
- Communicate deftly
- Demonstrate technical proficiency

Results of Succession Planning for the IC. *Source: Author.*

To resolve this problem and answer the question, the paper first reviewed leader and leadership literature for insight into the behaviors and abilities one might expect of IC leaders. An understanding of leaders, leadership, and succession literature may help IC succession planners avoid the pitfalls of whimsical leader requirements or the cloning of current managers. The examination of succession as a process revealed its basic components and the requisite environment for its realization. This study depicts the business case to be made, with attention to arguments for and against succession management. The statutory requirements for personnel management, and specifically for senior executives, indicate clear support for undertaking such a program. Interviews with senior IC professionals exposed the history and status of Community succession management.

The literature reviewed here *begins* to provide signposts for the adoption of succession management in the Community. Equally important, the literature points to questions that remain to be asked as procedural details take form.

Making It Stick

Our Leaders

People watch, and are prone to emulate, the behaviors of their leaders. No matter how eloquent, leaders' words are of less importance than their actions. If senior IC leaders believe implementation of succession management to be a critical activity for the Community, then they will exhibit behavior that makes that clear. Three ways senior leaders demonstrate support: 1) they dedicate sufficient resources to establish, maintain, and improve the process; 2) they participate in development and implementation of the process; and 3) they apply the process to the selection and placement of new leaders. [123]

Identifying staff and allocating essential resources would be likely launch activities for succession management development and implementation. Establishment of a team—a program management team—to investigate the work to be done, recommend the steps to select and prepare future leaders, and underscore major milestones along the way would be consistent with most of the literature as proof of commitment to the process. This team, empowered to act across the IC, would have clear, measurable, and published goals, including a reasonable schedule, accountability requirements, and per-

---

[123] U.S. Congress, House, Subcommittee on Civil Service and Agency Organization, Committee on Government Reform, *Posthearing Questions Related to Succession Planning and Management*, Hearings, 108th Cong., 1st sess., 14 November 2003, 3.

formance expectations. The team might take a programmatic approach to reinforce succession management implementation as a substantial, long-term undertaking. For example, management of schedules, requirements, and performance milestones can be presented in a formal Statement of Work (SOW) or a Work Breakdown Structure (WBS). Such a characterization establishes the perception of succession management implementation as a structured, manageable program, not just an "effort," a term frequently used as code for work with no substantial support or expected (or desired) results.

Although senior IC officials may designate a team or individual to define IC succession management, they themselves have the obligation to invest their own time and energy to make it effective and institutionalized. Much as *rumint* can become an employee's information source, *calendarint* can reveal a great deal about what leaders consider important. [124] All employees need do is scan a senior leader's calendar for time spent on succession activities or in meetings on the topic to know the corresponding level of commitment.

Another way to reinforce the importance of succession management is for senior leaders to use it. Seniors involved in selecting future leaders should exercise newly established succession procedures in making these choices. Over time, adjustments may be made to minimize the information processing or time requirements, but these should be made with improvement in mind, not as change for change's sake or accommodation. Significant thought should precede any exceptions to the rules. All changes should be thoroughly documented and explained with a strong supporting rationale. The workforce, stakeholders, and recruits will get the message that the IC takes seriously the process for effective leader preparation, selection, and placement when current leaders dedicate themselves to its use.

Ourselves

One of the most critical and earliest tasks for the IC succession development team may be that of gaining employees' enthusiastic support for succession management. Employees are well served by a fair and understandable process for advancement and development. The message may be well received, particularly if it can be crafted to assuage concerns about pay-for-performance changes already in the offing. Of concern, then, may be the unintended squeeze on middle managers and supervisors who will be expected to explain and help employees through the process while try-

---

124 *Rumint* is a term often used to refer to information gathered and exchanged as part of the flow of rumors. *Calendarint* refers to viewing an individual's on-line or desk top calendar to locate him/her, identify blocks of meeting time, or speculate about activities or visitors.

ing to work through it themselves. Part of the buy-in process must focus on explaining the front-line benefits to and the critical role played by managers.

> **Part of the buy-in process must focus on explaining the front-line benefits to and the critical role played by managers.**

An enticement may be their own stake in the process—their own development and opportunity for advancement, as well as enhanced performance of their workgroups. Even while working to gain endorsement from mid-level managers and supervisors, Community succession implementers must ensure that these individuals are held accountable for meeting the letter and intent of the process.

Drawing on Gladwell's premise that ideas spread in thoroughly "biological" fashion once a seed has been planted, ODNI and a succession development team might search for those who can propagate a succession management movement. Identification of individuals in senior ranks and their direct subordinates who can act as change agents for each agency and for the Community should be an early activity—either by the development team or by the DNI. This is not the identification of champions for the new process. Rather, it is gaining an understanding of who influences others within their own agencies to accept new ideas. Using Gladwell's term, these individuals will help create the "tipping point"[125] toward successful implementation.

And Now for Something Somewhat Different

Opportunities abound for more in-depth investigations of succession management and its implementation in the IC. The following represent just a few of those opportunities.

What's up with Gen X and Gen Y? Do younger employees really have very different concepts of career success than their predecessors?[126] The impact on IC missions, culture, and infrastructure from employees who may spend fewer years in one job, field, or agency could be dramatic. Their reputed expectations for intellectual challenge, feedback, and recognition need to be related to the concept of succession management. Results from the Gen Y Project, conducted under the auspices of ODNI's Leadership Development

---

125 Malcolm Gladwell, *The Tipping Point: How Little Things Can Make a Big Difference* (New York: Little, Brown and Company, 2000), 7.

126 Paul C. Light, "The Empty Government Talent Pool: The New Public Service Arrives," *The Brookings Review* 2000, 20-23

activities, may inform succession implementers about possible procedural, developmental, or outcomes definition changes.[127]

We both need to change…you first! An associated research area is that of cultural versus individual adjustment. It remains unclear how much the IC culture can and should change to fit the new workforce and workplace realities. Equally unclear, despite the literature reviewed for this paper, is the amount of adjustment new employees can and should expect to make to the organization's extant culture. Presumably, both must adjust. For the IC, insofar as it remains an entrenched bureaucracy, the flexibility required for it to act on the findings of academic studies and industry best practices may be limited. Industrial/Organizational psychology, not explored by this author, may harbor useful suggestions for adjusting the IC culture to the new employment realities.

Unknown unknowns about knowing. The present paper does provide some visibility into mechanisms for developing leaders knowledge through education, experience, and mentoring, but the broader field of knowledge management has additional application to the IC. As employees leave the workforce, they take with them not just training information, but the understanding of how and why organizations operate as they do. Additionally, mission-related knowledge, particularly the psychological understanding of adversaries gathered over time, may be lost when the current experts opt out of the IC. Research into knowledge transfer techniques or patterns may affect aspects of succession management, such as assignments (timing, type, expected learning) and mentoring (training for both mentors and mentees and participant matching).

Help the caterpillar become the butterfly. Although baby boomers have been expected to depart in large numbers, the rate of departure is slower than expected. It may be worth examining why these boomers are staying. If their departure would in fact be advantageous to the IC, research may show how to make that departure occur faster. Rather than forcing them out, it may be best to offer knowledge transfer and mentoring opportunities as a way to allow them a gradual adjustment to retirement while ensuring the continued success of the IC. This may require adjustments in succession management over the long-term—prioritization of positions or identification of transitional assignments. Some of the succession literature reviewed for the present paper does address this and similar areas.[128]

---

127 Developmental Testing Service LLC, *Gen Y Project Report*, 24 November 2006.

128 Sonnenfeld in *Leadership Succession*, 138.

Welcome back, Butterfly. A related topic for further consideration may be the current practice of rehiring retired senior executives. It may be valuable to learn about the impact of former senior executives on the succession process, particularly those retained as contractors within the organizations from which they retired. Legal requirements exist regarding the timing of their return; however, returnees may not be completely "out of the loop" as it remains unlikely that the entire management team would have changed in the period between retirement and return. One may hope that the influence of these experts would be strong on procedure modification, but their actual or perceived impact on leader selection should be monitored closely to ensure selection officials feel no undue influence, nor pressure to modify succession outcomes to satisfy former mentors.

> "Overall, the establishment of a solid succession management process delivers the same benefit that any good process provides: the ability to complete given tasks efficiently and effectively, and to use accurate data to make decisions and identify areas for improvement." [129]

"Process matters"

---

[129] "Succession Management: Filling the Leadership Pipeline," S1-4.

WORKS CONSULTED

"5 CFR Chapter 214, Senior Executive Service."

"5 CFR Chapter 317, Employment in the Senior Executive Service."

"5 U.S.C. Section 3132." GPO.

The 9/11 Commission Report: Final Report of the National Commission on Terrorist Attacks Upon the United States. July 2004.

A source, Member of the Society of Competitive Intelligence Professionals (SCIP). telephone interview by author, 15 February 2007.

A source, mid-level intelligence professional at a national intelligence organization, who wishes to remain anonymous. Interview by the author, 6 November 2006.

A source, senior-level intelligence professional at a national intelligence organization, who wishes to remain anonymous. Interview by the author, 8 November 2006.

A source, senior-level intelligence professional at a national intelligence organization, who wishes to remain anonymous. Interview by the author, 14 November 2006.

A source, senior-level intelligence professional at a national intelligence organization, who wishes to remain anonymous. Interview by the author, 6 February 2007.

A source, senior-level intelligence professional at a national intelligence organization, who wishes to remain anonymous. Interview by the author, 22 February 2007.

Auerback, Carl F., and Louise B. Silverstein. *Qualitative Data: An Introduction to Coding and Analysis.* New York: New York University Press, 2003.

Ayres-Williams, Roz. "Making Sure You Go the Distance: Show You've Planned for the Long Haul by Having a Succession Plan in Place." *Black Enterprise*, April 1998, 23.

Barger, Deborah G. *Toward a Revolution in Intelligence Affairs.* RAND, 2005.

WORKS CONSULTED (Continued)

Bass, Bernard M. *Bass & Stogdill's Handbook of Leadership: Theory, Research, and Managerial Applications.* 3rd ed. New York: The Free Press, 1990.

Bennett, Robert H. III, and others. "Today's Corporate Executive Leadership Programs: Building for the Future." *Journal of Leadership Studies* (1999): 3.

Bennis, Warren. *On Becoming a Leader.* Reading, MA: Addison-Wesley Publishing Company, 1989.

Bernthal, Paul, and Richard Wellins. "Trends in Leader Development and Succession." *Human Resource Planning* 29, no. 2 (2006): 31+.

Blair, Billie G. "Nothing Succeeds Like Succession Planning." *Security Management*, September 2005, 94+.

Blanchard, Benjamin S. and Wolter J. Fabrycky, *Systems Engineering and Analysis*, 2nd ed. Englewood Cliffs, NJ: Prentice Hall, 1990.

Bledsoe, Ralph, and others. *Building Successful Organizations: A Guide to Strategic Workforce Planning.* Washington, DC: National Academy of Public Administration Center for Human Resources Management, 2000. *http://www.napawash.org/publications.html.* Accessed 11 July 2006.

———. *Managing Succession and Developing Leadership: Growing the Next Generation of Public Service Leaders.* Washington, DC: National Academy of Public Administration, 1997. *http://www.napawash. org/publications.html. Accessed 11 July 2006.*

Burns, James MacGregor. *Leadership.* New York: Harper & Row, 1978.

Civil Service Reform Act of 1978. PL 95-454. 13 October.

Conlan, Carolyn. Director, IC Leadership Development Office (ODNI). Interview by the author, 24 October 2006.

Cope, Faye. "Current Issues in Selecting High Potentials." *Human Resource Planning* 21, no. 3 (1998): 15+.

Corporate Executive Board-Corporate Leadership Council. *Hallmarks of Leadership Success: Strategies for Improving Leadership Team Quality and Executive Readiness.* Report. CLC114916M01, October 2003.

WORKS CONSULTED (Continued)

Dennis, Anita. "Succession-Planning Dos and Don'ts: Who Will Take over When You're Ready to Retire? If You Don't Know, It's Time to Decide." *Journal of Accountancy* 199, no. 2 (2005): 47+.

DNI. 2006 IC Annual Employee Climate Survey. URL: *<http:// <http:// www.dni.gov/reports/20070502_IC_Survey_Results.pdf>*. 10 October 2007.

Donkin, Richard. "Time to Pay Attention to Management Succession " *The Financial Times*, 15 September 2005, 15.

Drucker, Peter F. *The Effective Executive*. New York: Harper & Row, 1966.

"Effective Succession Management." *Personnel Today*, 19 November 2002, 4.

Executive Core Qualifications. Washington, DC: Office of Personnel Management, URL: https://www.opm.gov/ses/ecq.asp. 1 February 2007.

Federal Workforce Flexibility Act of 2004. 108-411. 108th, 30 October 2004.

Friedman, Stewart D., ed. *Leadership Succession*. New Brunswick, NJ: Transaction Books, 1986.

Gen Y Project Report. 24 November 2006.

Gladwell, Malcolm. *The Tipping Point: How Little Things Can Make a Big Difference*. New York: Little, Brown and Company, 2000.

A Guide to Succession Management. Nova Scotia, Canada: Nova Scotia Public Service Commission, 2005. Link from URL: *<http://www. gov.ns.ca/psc/>*. Accessed 16 August 2006.

Gummesson, Evert. *Qualitative Methods in Management Research*. Revised ed. Newbury Park, CA: Sage Publications, 1991.

Gutjahr, Melanie M.H. *The Intelligence Archipelago: The Community's Struggle to Reform in the Globalized Era*. Washington, DC: Joint Military Intelligence College, 2005.

Gutteridge, Thomas G., and others. "A New Look at Organizational Career Development." *Human Resource Planning* 16, no. 2 (1993): 71+.

WORKS CONSULTED (Continued)

Harrell, Margaret C., and others. *Aligning the Stars: Improvements to General and Flag Officer Management.* Santa Monica, CA: RAND, 2004.

Harris, Shane. "Movin' on Up." *GOVEXEC.com,* 8 November 2006.

Hesselbein, Frances, and others, eds. *The Leader of the Future: New Visions, Strategies, and Practices for the Next Era.* San Francisco: Jossey-Bass, 1996.

Homeland Security Act of 2002. 107-296. 25 November.

Human Capital: Insights for U.S. Agencies from Other Countries' Succession Planning and Management Initiatives. GAO-03-914, 15 September 2003.

Human Capital: Nine Key Principles from Nine Private Sector Organizations. 31 January 2000.

Human Capital: Selected Agencies Have Opportunities to Enhance Existing Succession Planning and Management Efforts. GAO-05-585, 2005.

Ibarra, Patrick. "Succession Planning: An Idea Whose Time Has Come." *Public Management,* January-February 2005, 18+.

Ingraham, Patricia W., and others. *Strengthening Senior Leadership in the U.S. Government.* In *Phase I Report* Washington, DC: National Academy of Public Administration, 2000. *http://www.napawash. org/publications.html. Accessed 11 July 2006.*

Intelligence Reform and Terrorism Prevention Act of 2004. 108-458. 108th Congress, 2d Session, 17 December, 2004.

Jacoby, L. E., Vice Admiral, USN, and Louis Andre. *Revitalizing and Reshaping the Workforce: A White Paper from the Joint Staff J2.* Washington, DC: Department of Defense, 2000.

Johnston, Rob, PhD. *Analytic Culture in the U.S. Intelligence Community.* Washington, DC: Center for the Study of Intelligence, CIA, 2005.

Juran, J. M. *Juran on Leadership for Quality: An Executive Handbook.* New York: The Free Press, 1989.

WORKS CONSULTED (Continued)

Kellerman, Barbara. *Bad Leadership: What It Is, How It Happens, Why It Matters*. Boston, MA: Harvard Business School Press, 2004.

Kettl, Donald F., and others. *Civil Service Reform: Building a Government That Works*. Washington, DC: Brookings Institution Press, 1996.

Kouzes, James M., and Barry Z. Posner. *The Leadership Challenge*. 3rd rev. ed. San Francisco, CA: Jossey-Bass, 2002.

Kuhn, Thomas S. *The Structure of Scientific Revolutions*. Chicago, IL: The University of Chicago Press, 1996.

Lancaster, Lynne C., and David Stillman. "If I Pass the Baton, Who Will Grab It? Creating Bench Strength in Public Management." *Public Management*, September 2005, 8+.

Leibman, Michael and others. "Succession Management: The Next Generation of Succession Planning." *Human Resource Planning* 19, no. 3 (1996): 16+.

Light, Paul C. "The Empty Government Talent Pool: The New Public Service Arrives." *The Brookings Review* 2000, 20-23.

Major, James S. *Citation: Note and Bibliographic Form*. 2nd ed. Washington, DC: Defense Intelligence Agency, Joint Military Intelligence College, 2003.

_____. *Style: Usage, Composition, and Form*. 2nd ed. Washington, DC: Defense Intelligence Agency, Joint Military Intelligence College, 2004.

Manz, Charles C., and Henry P. Sims, Jr. *Superleadership: Leading Others to Lead Themselves*. New York: Prentiss Hall Press, 1989.

McConnell, Michael. Office of the Director of National Intelligence. *United States Intelligence Community (IC): 100 Day Plan for Integration and Collaboration*. 2007.

McFee, Thomas S., and others. *Developing the Leadership Team: An Agency Guide*. 21st Century Federal Manager Series, December 2003.

_____. *Final Report and Recommendations: The 21st Century Federal Manager*. 21st Century Federal Manager Series, February 2004.

WORKS CONSULTED (Continued)

_____. *Leadership for Leaders: Senior Executives and Middle Managers. 21st Century Federal Manager Series*, August 2003.

Merriam-Webster Online Dictionary, Online Ed., 2005. URL: <http://www.m-w.com/dictionary>. Accessed 12 April 2007.

Miller, Lynn. "Initiative for Self-Development Identifies Future Leaders." *HRMagazine*, January 2001, 20.

National Security Act of 1947. PL 80-253. 26 July.

The Next Generation: Accelerating the Development of Rising Leaders. Corporate Leadership Council, 1997.

Office of Personnel Management. *Federal Human Capital Survey 2006*. URL: <http//www.fhcs2006.opm.gov>. Accessed 13 August 2007.

Office of the Director of National Intelligence, *IC Annual Employee Climate Survey: IC Survey 2006, Survey Results* (Office of the Intelligence Community Chief Human Capital Officer (CHCO): March 2007). Attachment to e-mail from Stephen J. Kerda, Member NDIC Staff, to NDIC Staff (alias), 19 April 2007.

"Oracle Web Page." 2007.

_____. *Human Capital Assessment and Accountability Framework*. Web-only tools and information. 2007. URL: <*http://apps.opm.gov/HumanCapital/tool/indes.cfm*>. Accessed 23 January 2007.

Pernick, Robert. "Creating a Leadership Development Program: Nine Essential Tasks." *Public Management*, August 2002, 10+.

"Plateau Systems Unveils Industry's First Enterprise-Class Ondemand Performance, Learning, and Succession Management Solution; Expanded Offering Will Provide Companies with Flexible and Affordable Best-in-Class Talent Management Solution." *Business Wire*, 13 June 2006.

"Research by Develop. Dimensions Inter. Gives Tips on Corporate Succession Management." *Daily Record*, 17 December 2001.

Robb, Drew. "Succeeding with Succession: Tools for Succession Management Get More Sophisticated." *HR Magazine*, January 2006, 89-92.

WORKS CONSULTED (Continued)

Rothwell, William J., PhD, SPHR. *Effective Succession Planning.* 3rd ed. New York: American Management Association (AMACOM), 2005.

Schall, Ellen. "Public Sector Succession: A Strategic Approach to Sustaining Innovation." *Public Administration Review* 57, no. 1 (1997): 4+.

Schein, Edgar H. *Organizational Culture and Leadership* San Francisco, CA: Jossey-Bass Publishers, 1985.

Senge, Peter M. *The Fifth Discipline: The Art & Practice of the Learning Organization.* New York, NY: Currency Doubleday, 1990.

Smith, Christine. "Eagan Minnesota: Growth with Grace." *Public Management*, December 2005, 32+.

Smith, Eleanor M., and others. *A Preliminary Evaluation of the NRO Succession Management Program.* 477, September 2004.

Sources, senior-level professionals at OPM, who wish to remain anonymous. Interview by the author, 31 January 2007.

"Succession Management: Filling the Leadership Pipeline." *Chief Executive* (U.S.), April 2004, S1-4.

"Succession Planning Facts and Fantasies." *Journal for Quality & Participation*, 22 September 2005, 4-6.

Torres, Roselinde, and William Pasmore. "How to Successfully Manage CEO Succession." *Corporate Board* 26, no. 152 (2005): 1-10.

U.S. Congress, House, Subcommittee on Civil Service and Agency Organization, Committee on Government Reform. *Posthearing Questions Related to Succession Planning and Management.* Hearings, 108th Cong., 1st sess., 14 November 2003.

U.S. Congress, House, Subcommittee on Civil Service and Agency Reorganization, Committee on House Government Reform. *Improving Productivity of Federal Workforce.* Hearings, 108th Cong., 1st sess., 1 October 2003.

U.S. Congress, Joint Hearings, Subcommittee on Oversight of Government Management, Restructuring and the District of Columbia, Committee on Governmental Affairs, Senate, and Subcommittee

WORKS CONSULTED (Continued)

on Civil Service and Agency Organization, Committee on Government Reform, House, *Human Capital: Major Human Capital Challenges at the Departments of Defense and State.* Hearings, 107th Cong., 1st sess., 29 March 2001.

U. S. Congress, Senate. *Intelligence Reform and Terrorism Prevention Act of 2004.* 108th Cong., 2d session, 2004. S.2845.

The U.S. Intelligence Community's Five Year Strategic Human Capital Plan. Office of the Director of National Intelligence, 2006.

U.S. President, Executive Order 11315. *"Amending the Civil Service Rules to Authorize an Executive Assignment System for Positions in Grades 16, 17, and 18 of the General Schedule".* Federal Register, 1966.

_____. *Executive Order 11348. "Providing for the Further Training of Government Employees."* Federal Register, 1967.

_____. *President's Management Agenda.* Washington, DC: Office of the White House, 2002.

Walker, James W. "Do We Need Succession Planning Anymore?" *Human Resource Planning* 21, no. 3 (1998): 9+.

Walker, James W., and James M. LaRocco. "Succession Management and the Board." *Corporate Board*, Jan-Feb 2004, 10-16.

Wren, Thomas J. *The Leader's Companion: Insights on Leadership through the Ages.* New York: The Free Press, 1995.

Zaccaro, Stephen J. *Models and Theories of Executive Leadership: A Conceptual/Empirical Review and Integration.* U.S. Army Research Institute for the Behavioral and Social Sciences, 1996.

_____. *The Nature of Executive Leadership: A Conceptual and Empirical Analysis of Success.* Washington, DC: American Psychological Association, 2001.

Zaccaro, Stephen J., and Richard J. Klimoski, eds. *The Nature of Organizational Leadership: Understanding the Performance Imperatives Confronting Today's Leaders, The Organizational Frontiers.* San Francisco: Jossey-Bass, 2001.

ABOUT THE AUTHOR

The author has been an Intelligence Community employee at the National Security Agency (NSA) for 20 years. Certified as an information systems security analyst, she has worked in the Information Assurance, Signals Intelligence, and Acquisition organizations. In addition to serving at the Pentagon and overseas, she was an American Political Science Association (APSA) Congressional Fellow. She holds a BA in French and an MS in systems engineering. She is currently assigned to NSA's Associate Directorate for Education and Training.

Science is continuing search; it is continuing generation of theories, models, concepts, and categories. It is realistic to view research as a journey in which each program represents a temporary stop on the way, and where each report is a point of departure for further inquiry. [130]

---

130 Evert Gummesson, *Qualitative Methods in Management Research*, rev. ed. (Newbury Park, CA: Sage Publications, 1991), 18.

www.ingramcontent.com/pod-product-compliance
Lightning Source LLC
Chambersburg PA
CBHW072106280526
45788CB00006B/2423